THE WAY OF WYRD

I awoke suddenly with a start. It was still dark and I felt that I had been asleep only a few moments. I tried to collect my thoughts for I knew now what I must do: it was the Will of the Almighty that I go with Wulf and learn the ways of his spirits. And as soon as the resolve passed into my mind, I felt an uncanny sense of security and well-being. The terrors of the night were extinguished like snuffed candles. I thought at first that I was enjoying the relief of having made the decision, but gradually it dawned upon me that I was feeling the excitement of anticipation. It was not just a matter of duty or loyalty to Eappa, nor even the undoubted joy of serving the Lord. Rather, the secrets of the spirits seemed to beckon to me and the surrounding forest tingled with excitement and challenge. Above, the pagan sky floated blue as turquoise, silver stars twinkling like jewelled icons and the moon pouring down light like a heaven full of altar candles. The thunder god had withdrawn and the Lord was blessing my Mission.

THE
Way of Wyrd

TALES OF AN
ANGLO-SAXON SORCERER

BRIAN BATES

ARROW BOOKS ·

Arrow Books Limited
62–65 Chandos Place, London WC2N 4NW

An imprint of Century Hutchinson Ltd

London Melbourne Sydney Auckland
Johannesburg and agencies throughout
the world

First published in Great Britain by
Century Publishing Co. Ltd 1983

First paperback publication by
Century Publishing Co. Ltd 1984
Arrow edition 1986

Printed and bound in Great Britain by
The Guernsey Press Co. Ltd, Guernsey, C.I.

ISBN 0 09 947790 4

TO BETH, PEARL AND ROBIN

CONTENTS

PREFACE

MIDDLE-EARTH is a term which evokes the time and culture of Anglo-Saxon, Icelandic and Norse Europe: a time of saga, spirits and sorcery. This book documents the teachings of a sorcerer from that culture, a spirit-diviner and mystic who practised his art in Anglo-Saxon England. His views of life and death, psychological and paranormal powers, omens and journeys into the spirit-world, are chronicled by an apprentice who was the direct recipient of his knowledge. The book recreates and makes accessible a remarkable path to psychological and spiritual liberation; a way of being in the world that challenges our very notions of body, mind and spirit. I believe the teachings of the Way of Wyrd to be as potent and challenging today as they were a thousand years ago.

I am a psychologist and this book is a report of a major research project into the nature of Anglo-Saxon sorcery. Although the book tells the compelling story of a sorcerer and his apprentice it is not strictly a work of fiction, for the mission, historical settings, sequence of events, details of the teachings – even the character of Wulf, the sorcerer – are reconstructed from research evidence. A bibliography of the main sources is provided at the end of the book. *The Way of Wyrd* had its beginnings in the early 1970s when I was researching, both as a psychologist and in my personal life, the teachings of Zen and Tao. But I soon became interested in discovering Western parallels to these remarkable Eastern traditions, for it seems to me that every culture has at some time in its history evolved teachings and techniques which enable individuals to transcend the layers of conventional reality to experience a separate vision: a dimension in which our notions of time, space and causality are suspended. I began searching for a Western tradition which might encompass some of the perspectives of the East.

After some interesting but false starts in alchemy and medieval witchcraft, I came upon a thousand-year-old manuscript from the Anglo-Saxon period, preserved in the British Museum (ms Harley 585). It is a collection of magical/medical remedies probably recorded by Christian monks in the tenth century, but reflecting a tradition several hundred years earlier. In contrast with other monastic collections, which were usually translations of classical medical texts from the Greek, this particular manuscript records the medical practices of pagan practitioners operating within the indigenous Anglo-Saxon culture. Each magical/medical remedy has one or more of the following features: a plant-based concoction to be applied to the patient, a set of rituals associated with the treatment, and an incantation, spell or charm to be sung as part of the treatment. In the text of these magical remedies, I saw the possibilities of finding a Western spiritual tradition containing some of the features of the systems of the East.

The medical manuscript has been translated into modern English several times by Anglo-Saxon scholars, but has never been subjected to the depth of psychological analysis that formed the basis of this research project. Using the medical remedies as a focus, I began research in two directions. The first was to build a picture of the world in which the Anglo-Saxon sorcerer lived and worked, a task which led me into areas as far afield as the history of medicine, comparative mythology, Anglo-Saxon archaeology, folklore, Old English literature and, of course, the social history of the so-called 'Dark Ages'. The second line of research concerned humanistic and transpersonal theories of psychological development, altered states of consciousness and psychological studies of traditional Eastern spiritual disciplines. The evidence very quickly confirmed that in a then very heavily forested land, populated by perhaps one million people divided into small, competing kingdoms, there thrived a powerful tradition of sorcery and mysticism. Individual sorcerers practised healing and divination, presided over worship rituals and festivals, and sometimes served as advisers to the kings. Most importantly, analysis of the evidence has revealed that the teachings, beliefs, practices and ways of initiation of Anglo-Saxon sorcery constituted a Western way of psychological and spiritual liberation.

By AD 1000 the sorcerers and mystics of the indigenous population had been largely replaced by Christian missionaries, at least in the official circles of courts and kings, although of course the popular appeal of the traditional ways survived for a further several hundred years. The women practitioners – sorceresses who had for the most part been ignored by the original Christian missionaries – continued to flourish for so long that, several hundred years later, the institutionalised church had to mount the now infamous witch-hunting trials in an effort to control their activities.

Elements of Anglo-Saxon sorcery and mysticism survive today only in fragmentary form, but similar concepts and perspectives are undergoing a dramatic resurgence in the last third of this century, particularly in the areas of medicine and healing, meditation and mysticism, parapsychology and personal transformation, ecology, and most recently in theoretical developments in the physical and natural sciences. Much of the work in these areas has profited from the teachings of the great Eastern spiritual traditions, which complement our scientific and technological developments in important ways. I believe that we may equally well enrich our notions of life and of being in the world by travelling in time into our own cultural past as by travelling in miles to study distant cultural traditions. *The Way of Wyrd* is a path to knowledge that offers teachings, concepts, perspectives and experiences that speak to us with a provocative and compelling relevance to contemporary existence.

While the reader may find within this book teachings of personal significance, there are a number of general and far-reaching dimensions of *The Way of Wyrd* which are immediately apparent. Most fundamentally, the Middle-Earth sorcerer lived out a view of life called *wyrd*: a way of being which transcends our conventional notions of free will and determinism. All aspects of the world were seen as being in constant flux and motion between the psychological and mystical polarities of Fire and Frost: a creative, organic vision paralleling the classical Eastern concepts of Yin and Yang, and echoed by recent developments in theoretical physics in which the world is conceived of as relationships and patterns. Following from the concept of *wyrd* was a vision of the universe, from the gods to the underworld, as being connected by an enormous all-reaching system of fibres rather like a three-dimensional spider's web. Everything was connected by strands of fibre to the all-encompassing web. Any event, anywhere, resulted in reverberations and repercussions throughout the web. This image far surpasses in ambition our present views of ecology, in which we have extended our notions of cause and effect to include longer and more lateral chains of influence in the natural world. The web of fibres of the Anglo-Saxon sorcerer offers an ecological model which encompasses individual life events as well as general physical and biological phenomena, non-material as well as material events, and challenges the very cause and effect chains upon which our ecological theories depend.

The Anglo-Saxon sorcerer dealt directly with *life-force*, a vital energy which permeated everything but which in humans was generated in the head, flowed down the spinal column and from there throughout the body. This system of energy, which has intriguing similarities to Eastern concepts of prana and chi, encapsulated physical, psychological and spiritual domains within a single, unified system. The manipulation of *life-force* was central to the sorcerers' healing work, and has implications for much of the contemporary debate in holistic medicine concerning mind/body interaction, healing energies, and complementary approaches to health. *Life-force* connected individual human functioning with the pulse of earth rhythm, a psychological and spiritual dimension of life which has been excluded by our technological cocoon.

A dynamic and pervasive world of *spirits* coexisted with the material world in Anglo-Saxon culture. The spirits, manifestations of forces pertaining to *wyrd*, were invisible to most humans, although they played a prominent and superstitious role in the everyday lives of Anglo-Saxons. But the spirits were visible to the sorcerers, because sorcerers were people naturally endowed with perceptual abilities beyond the normal; abilities to see, hear and experience things which we would probably consign to the realms of the paranormal or madness. These abilities were recognised, cultivated and nurtured as evidence of a person's fitness for admission to the world of sorcery. The sorcerer dealt directly with spirits, and operated as a mediator between the world of humans and the realm of spirits. The Anglo-Saxon spirits seemed to give identity and form to many phenomena in life which contemporary psychology recognises but often fails to deal with directly: coincidence, deep seated fears, psychic experiences, prophetic dreams and nightmares and other aspects of ourselves that remain unconscious. Recent developments in existential psychiatry and the new psychotherapies have begun to look for ways of working directly with these forces.

There is, of course, an enormous gulf between the psychological worlds of Anglo-Saxon and contemporary societies. Yet there are enduring features of human existence which seem to change little with the passage of time, and it is to these facets of life that a past philosophy can speak with clarity and relevance. *The Way of Wyrd* is a work of psychological archaeology, but I believe it to be more than of merely historical interest. As a way of personal transformation with philosophical and spiritual power, it strikes to the heart of many contemporary concerns with the vitality of a living system.

In researching Anglo-Saxon sorcery and mysticism, I pulled apart and examined the many strands of evidence in conventional scientific fashion. It was a process of rigorous analysis which gradually revealed the dimensions and psychological parameters of Anglo-Saxon sorcery. But in writing this book, I wished to present a vital sense of the whole; to reconstruct and make accessible the Way of Wyrd in a form which would provide some sense of this organic, holistic, spiritual approach to life and power. I chose, then, to present the research in the form of a documentary novel in which each event and detail of the teachings is reconstructed from the Anglo-Saxon evidence.

In constructing the book, I first mapped out the sequence of events which characterised a typical process of training and initiation, culled from Anglo-Saxon material and confirmed by comparative evidence from other disciplines. Each facet of the teaching, element of the philosophy and significant event was anchored to a specific segment of Anglo-Saxon material. The evidence was analysed and then written out into narrative form. Each chapter in the book represents my interpretation and commentary on a particular dimension of the Anglo-Saxon material. All along I endeavoured to remain faithful to the primary data for Anglo-Saxon sorcery; comparative evidence was used to investigate and analyse, but not to impose meanings.

Then, to bring the material to life, I set it against the imagined story of how one man was led into the world of the Anglo-Saxon sorcerer. In choosing an appropriate story, which would carry all the documentary evidence I had prepared, I went back to the original *Lacnunga* manuscript with which I had begun my investigations. Historians have suggested that the original author of the Anglo-Saxon magical/medical manuscript was a scribe or cleric attached to a Christian monastery. I therefore took as the background of the book a historically documented mission which in the late 600s travelled to the still pagan south coast of England. I have told the story of *The Way of Wyrd* through the eyes of a scribe attached to the mission; a man whom I imagine to be the original creator of the *Lacnunga* manuscript. This book documents a Western way of spiritual liberation by chronicling the path the author of the *Lacnunga* might have followed in gathering his material – by becoming a sorcerer's apprentice and entering *The Way of Wyrd*.

PART ONE

The Way of Wyrd

1

THE SORCERER'S SPIRIT
CIRCLE

'WASTE-DWELLER, why do you spin your spell?'

The sorcerer's voice rasped from gaping fangs as he crouched over the sick woman like a giant wolf-man. He looked awesome, wrapped in an enormous grey wolf-skin, the wolf-head resting on top of his own so that he towered at least seven feet tall.

The Spirit House was crowded with the entire population of the settlement, including children and even babes-in-arms, but no one moved or made a sound. People sat still as carved icons, fire-shadows dancing on faces crammed three deep around the walls. Inside the Spirit Circle, bounded by ropes suspended from stakes pounded into the earth floor, only I sat next to the sorcerer, dry-mouthed, gripped by the imminent presence of the pagan powers of darkness.

Firelight crawled over the giant wolf-skin, glowed on the snake-clasp at the sorcerer's throat and brought the gold-wrought eyes of the wolf-head glittering into life. Slowly, carefully, the sorcerer settled into an attacking position opposite the woman, humping his back like a hunting wolf. The woman sat stiff and straight-backed, her scrawny body clamped by fear. Her head bobbed and weaved to avoid the Wolfman's glinting eyes until, twitching, she dropped her head and stared at the ground as if spellbound by the floor straw. In the smoky light I could see the grotesque growth at the bridge of her nose and the flesh around her eye, puffy and angry with infection.

Abruptly the Wolfman howled, hoarse with emotion:

'Spirit, why do you dwell on this woman's face? You have

snatched this woman's soul and left your battle-scars on her face. Without her soul this woman is dying. Where are you now? Where do you lurk, nursing her soul like a flesh-ripping carrion eater? Are you prowling the forest like a dealer in death? Are you on Dodda's Ridge? Grendel's Pit? Eagle Mountain? Or are you lying low, like a wounded fox, in stagnant ditchwater? For an evil sickness, voyaging far from home, you have outstayed your welcome. Wherever you are hiding, I shall hunt you down!'

There was a short silence, punctuated only by the hiss and snap of the fire. Suddenly, without warning, the sorcerer ripped off the wolf-skin and rolled into a hunched shape next to the woman, his back humped and head pressed between his knees, his elbows projecting out from his sides.

'Leave me alone,' he said, in a high, shrill voice.

Astonished, I darted a furtive glance around the room; serious faces watched the proceedings intently and I choked back a nervous laugh

The sorcerer leapt back into his wolf-skin.

'Leave you alone?' he snarled, stalking menacingly back and forth in front of the woman. 'You are leaving, banished to the Land of the Dead from whence you came!'

He threw off the wolf-skin and jumped back into his humped position.

'What are you going to do?' he squeaked, again impersonating the wart-shape.

The Wolfman leapt to his feet, his eyes flashing like dragon-flame before they disappeared beneath the wolf-head.

'I am going to hunt you down,' he howled.

The crumpled wart-shape again stared at the empty wolf-skin.

'Why are you hunting me?' it squeaked. 'Who summoned you?'

'Worthy spirits summoned me, for you are a burden. You are a waste-dweller trespassing where you are not wanted. You are a menace, to be driven out,' ranted the Wolfman, strutting around the Spirit Circle, the massive wolf-skin swaying from side to side.

I glanced back at the woman's face, almost anticipating a reply from the little wen sitting imperiously on her nose. In a mead hall the charade would have been greeted with roars of laughter as worthy drinking entertainment, but in the smoky Spirit Circle the proceedings were haunted by the choking chill of danger.

The Wolfman turned his attention back to the woman. Squatting in front of her, he slipped a hand inside the wolf-skin and, like a conjuror, produced a beaded leather strap. He handed this to me and pointed towards the woman's head.

I scrambled to my feet and knelt behind the woman in order to tie back her long hair. I had been expecting such a task for, though totally alien to such rituals, I was sitting inside the Spirit Circle as the sorcerer's assistant. But suddenly becoming the centre of attention terrified me and my hands trembled like the limbs of a frightened rabbit. The woman's hair slipped out of the loop before I could tighten the knot and the audience stirred impatiently, pushing against the hemp-rope barrier of the Spirit Circle. Blinking sweat from my eyes, I tried again; this time the knot held and I tied it back firmly.

Again the sorcerer dipped into the wolf-skin and this time produced a large linen sack from which he drew handfuls of spiky leaves, still fresh and green. Quickly and skilfully he folded them together, intertwining the stems, and rubbed them vigorously between his palms. I could hear him murmuring in a strange, high-pitched voice, as if he were singing to himself.

'Little wen, little wen, you have stolen this woman's soul. She is now as hollow as a rotten tree, but not for long, not for long.'

He padded softly up to the woman and tipped his head on one side, the glittering eyes of the wolf-skin glowing craftily. Then he addressed the spirit in a high, wheedling tone.

'Little wen, you should return home to the waste-lands, where you will be happy.'

Suddenly he slapped the pack of crushed leaves directly on to the woman's face and she swayed back with the impact. The Wolfman glanced at me sharply and I moved quickly behind the woman to give her support, holding her head in my hands.

Sitting back on his haunches and pushing the leaves against the woman's face with his left hand, the sorcerer slowly raised his right arm above his head: rows of eyes flashed in the firelight, following the gradual rise of his empty hand and watching his white fingers spreading apart above the wolf-skin. Suddenly his hand held a large object. A gasp whistled around the packed darkness and my stomach lurched sickeningly for he was grasping the enormous claw of a bird. Three huge, black eagle talons glowing menacingly in the flickering firelight.

The sorcerer moved the claw slowly towards the woman's face. Her eyes must have been open, for I could feel her head straining to keep the approaching object in her line of vision. She began to tremble violently and when the hideous stump touched her she whined and whimpered like a sick dog. Clamping the leaves on to the woman's face with the eagle claw, the Wolfman began a strange writhing, crawling dance, his body weaving slowly, silently, the wolf eyes locked to the woman's face. He chanted again, his words a wet cackle,

> *I begin my singing,*
> *and begin my chanting.*
> *Mighty spirit sitting at earth's rim,*
> *wrapped in eagle feathers,*
> *Mighty wind-winger,*
> *Stallion of the sky,*
> *Lend me your power*
> *that fares over Middle-Earth*
> *and the affairs of men.*

His voice reverberated inside my head like a chanted Mass and the room began to spin before my eyes. The Wolfman's voice faded to a hoarse whisper,

> *My words wing from Eagle-Spirit,*
> *Sharp-eyed dealer of death . . .*
> *Under the Eagle's claw may you wither,*
> *Under the Eagle's claw may you dry and drain*
> *Like barley in a bail, and water in a pail.*
> *May you become as small as linseed grain,*
> *And become so small that you become*
> *Nothing at all.*

Silently, like a spectre, the humped wart-shape appeared at the Wolfman's side. I thought that my eyes were playing tricks and shook my head to clear the dual image, but the wart-shape remained, not moving or breathing but staring directly at the Wolfman. I had not even had time to take in the physical appearance of the monster when suddenly the Wolfman shivered, jerked violently and was thrown to the ground, the eagle's claw dropping from his hand. The room burst into uproar and immediately the spirit shape disappeared. The Wolfman's body convulsed and writhed dangerously close to the fire, and I scrambled over to him and forced my right leg between him and the fire as a barrier. The sorcerer's body was bent backwards like a hunting bow and under the wolf-head his face gleamed woad-blue as he gasped and gurgled for every breath. Feverishly I struggled to snap open the snake clasp which secured the wolf-skin around his throat, but it was stuck fast. Desperately I whirled around, peering through swirling fire-smoke for help, but at that instant the sorcerer's knees slammed into his chest, shot away from him and he sprang to his feet like a willow whip. The heat of the fire burned into my leg and I jumped away with a yelp. I crawled back to my place on the edge of the Spirit Circle, watching the Wolfman in utter astonishment and unable to believe that his desperate choking had been merely an act.

Stepping away from the woman, the sorcerer paced around the fire again and began to hum. The audience fell silent immediately. Barely audible at first, the Wolfman's humming rose higher and higher in pitch, then became loud, harsh and plaintive, as if he were pleading with someone. People around the packed room took up the refrain the Wolfman had established, the humming gradually rising and falling with increasing power, the sounds vibrating against the walls and echoing into the roof-beams. Soon the audience began to sway back and forth, clapping in time to the rhythms, the smoke from the fire seeming to break up the movement of their bodies into small staccato jerks. The effect was spellbinding. I raised my hands and began to clap with everyone else.

While the noise continued unabated, the sorcerer turned back towards the woman. He seemed to have changed tactics. Squatting purposefully in front of her, he took another linen bag from inside the wolf-skin. Pulling open the drawstring, he carefully tipped out about a dozen irregularly shaped stones, each about the size of a man's fist, and arranged them on the gound, apparently laying them out in a set pattern or sequence. When he had finished I could see that each adjacent stone interlocked with neighbouring cavities to form an unbroken ring.

The sorcerer reached again into the sack and brought out a small glazed pot, painted with a mass of angular symbols, which he placed carefully in the centre of the small stone circle. Each movement was carefully controlled and precise, even elegant, and utterly compelling. Not once did I take my eyes off him.

A third time the sorcerer reached into the linen bag and this time pulled out a small pouch of the type used for storing finger rings. He picked open the knots on a drawstring threaded with tiny beads and poured the contents of the pouch into the glazed pot. Then he dipped a taper into the fire until it popped into flame and, slowly and deliberately, passed the burning taper back and forth over the bowl. The taper went out. All around me the clapping and humming crashed rhythmically into my ears, as the Wolfman relit the taper and again applied it to the bowl. Wreathes of copper-coloured smoke spiralled slowly from the circle of small stones; immediately he discarded the taper, leaned over and blew steadily into the bowl. He exhaled powerfully, hissing like a striking snake, and the burning power-plants crackled, popped and glowed deep red, smoke pungent as altar incense billowing into the air. The smoke drifted around my head like a shroud and I sniffed at it cautiously. At once the hairs inside my nose prickled and stiffened as if frozen by a winter frost, and I felt a tightness in my throat. My eyes began to stream tears and a moment later my ears buzzed and hummed. It was a disturbingly powerful sensation, and I shut my eyes tightly in an effort to regain control of my senses.

When I opened my eyes, the sorcerer was leaning directly over the smoking substance, his face close to the bowl, breathing deeply and rhythmically. Incredibly, the wolf-skin expanded and contracted like a weapon-smith's bellows as he pumped his body full of the orange smoke. I watched in horrified fascination, my head still floating from the merest whiff of the smoke. I could not conceive how he could fill his lungs with it.

The Wolfman exhaled into the bowl with a long, slow, controlled hiss, took one more mighty breath and gradually, his body trembling with effort, slowly raised himself to a sitting position. His lips were clamped tightly shut and his face and throat swelled like those of a bullfrog until I thought he would burst. He sat rigidly, staring unblinking into the firelight, his eyes glistening and streaming.

Suddenly the sorcerer's mouth snapped open and he belched streams of smoke like an enraged dragon. Immediately the humming and clapping ceased. The only sounds were the crackle of the fire and the heavy breathing of the packed audience, sounding like some monstrous, trapped animal.

Someone brought the Wolfman a bowl of water and he rose to his feet and stepped jerkily around the fire, drinking noisily, wisps of smoke escaping in thin streams from the corners of his mouth. He went around the rope perimeter three times, drinking the water, then discarded the bowl and picked up a very large linen sack he had placed near the blanket. He drew from it bundles of large green leaves and flung them onto the fire. The smothered flames hissed, red embers glowed balefully through heaps of greenery and streams of smoke surged, swirling towards the thatch. The sorcerer sat down. In the sudden gloom I could see his black, motionless figure in front of the fire, staring into the embers. He hiccoughed loudly once, then again and the entire wolf-skin shivered.

People behind me stirred and, under cover of virtual darkness, shifted position but the atmosphere in the dramatic setting still crackled with anticipation. Suddenly the sorcerer started talking, his voice loud and jerky, seeming to shudder from his body rather than coming from his mouth. I strained to understand what he was saying, but either he was making up the sounds or the strange dialect was too alien for me to follow. Then his utterances became more melodious, almost singing, though his voice retained an eerie, distant quality – rising, falling, trembling. There were lulls when his voice faded almost to a whisper, followed by great bursts of chatter, intense, rapid speaking, screeches, laughter and groans. He yawned, belched, chuckled and clapped his hands in time to his interminable sing-song. Gradually the Wolfman quietened down and the only sounds he made were hiccoughs and occasional mutterings; eventually even those subsided. Silence. I hardly dared to breathe.

Suddenly, without warning, the silence was shattered by loud cawing sounds as if a raven were swooping over our heads. I jumped with alarm, staring wildly about me in the darkness. Then came chirpings, whistles and cries as if the room had been invaded by hundreds of birds of every description, followed shortly after by the wailing of a baby awakened by the noise. I sat absolutely petrified.

The sorcerer's voice cut through the tumult and all sounds ceased instantly. Flames began to lick through the foliage strewn on the fire, sizzling and steaming, and soon the air was thick with an astringent aroma. The sorcerer rose and began to turn in a circle, slowly at first, barely moving his feet, but his voice was strong and resonant.

> *The spirits are here.*
> *Eagle-spirit you have come*
> *to take me where dead men dwell*
> *I shall enter all alone, wolf-bold,*
> *to retrieve the woman's lost soul.*

The sorcerer began twirling around in a circle, still slowly at first, then faster and faster, until he spun like a whirlwind, the only sound the rhythmic thump of his foot on the ground as he spun on the other. His wolf-skin flailed around him, whipping and snapping, tail flying like a hunting wolf charging in for the kill, voice rising to a higher pitch.

> *I run along with blinding speed,*
> *and fly over the waving fields of corn,*
> *looking down along the rivers,*
> *topping hills and treetops tall,*
> *through sailing clouds through the stars,*
> *into the land of the Mighty Ones.*

He dropped to a crouch. The fire spluttered as flames fought through the fresh, choking foliage. The gigantic wolf-shape began to glide around the fire, head and neck scooped low and I watched in awe; he seemed to have grown bigger and bigger while singing, until now, enormous, he filled the entire Spirit Circle, with the audience crammed back against the walls.

> *Now, we plunge down, down, down*
> *towards the ground,*
> *over moon shadows marching*
> *in giants' footsteps*

across the land.
I see below me in a crop field
a sick woman's soul in corn-spirits' hands.

He crouched absolutely motionless, back and hind-quarters hunched and fell silent. Nobody moved. Holding my breath, I shifted my gaze slowly over the room. The firelight splashed a red glow over stones, feathers and other objects festooned along the entire length of the rope, and above I saw flame flashes of sweating faces and attentive, unblinking eyes.

Suddenly the Wolfman leapt into the air with a howl and staggered around the Spirit Circle snarling and growling, seeming to totter on hind legs, the bright eyes of the wolf-head blazing blood-lust. His right arm stretched high over his head, above the wolf-skin. I squinted up into dark roof thatch and saw a long stalk of corn appear as if from nowhere, grasped in his hand.

A whining voice rasped:

> *Corn spirit, I have you,*
> *My fangs pierce your flesh*
> *Your battle armour is rent and torn,*
> *Your nine layers will be stripped,*
> *and when the last is put to flames,*
> *this woman's soul will be free.*

The corn stalk bobbed and weaved high in the air as the sorcerer moved around the circle. The voice snarled again:

> *Nine were corn spirit's layers,*
> *Nine layers of power,*
> *Nine were the links of armour*
> *But nine now I lower.*
> *Nine becomes eight!*

He tore off an ear of corn with his free hand, wheeled around the fire, and flung it into the flames.

'And eight becomes seven.'

'He tore off another ear and threw it into the fire.

'And seven becomes six.'

The corn stalk whipped and cracked above the Wolfman's head,

'And the six becomes five.'

As the next ear of corn sizzled into the flames I heard the word 'five' on the lips of people around me.

'And the five becomes four.'

This time the room rumbled with voices chanting, but then, to my horror, the corn stalk began to flail about in the sorcerer's hand as if it had a life of its own, the violence of its movement flinging him around the Spirit Circle. I shrank back against the rope to avoid his staggering feet,

'And the four becomes three.'

The audience roared approval as another ear of corn smacked into the flames, while the Wolfman clung on grimly to the cornstalk, his whirling wolf-cloak dispersing fire-smoke until my eyes streamed.

I tried to keep focus on the cornstalk's desperate struggle to escape his grasp.

'And the three becomes two.'

People behind me screamed the words with the sorcerer and pushed against the rope; I had to brace my feet and lean back to avoid being pitched into the fire.

'And the two becomes one.'

The audience roared as the Wolfman was literally thrown around the Spirit Circle, his wolf-head fangs snarling and growling, saliva flying in a foaming spray from the jaws.

'And the one becomes none,' he shrieked, tearing off a final kernel and dashing it into the flames. The cornstalk wrenched itself free at last and plunged screaming into the fire.

The crowded room exploded into uproar and at the same time the woman's head pitched forward out of my hands. She half rose, spinning around towards me; then the Wolfman swooped down, snatched away the leaf-pack still clinging to her face and flung it into the fire. Grasping the woman's arms, he hauled her to her feet, while the audience stood as one and I rose with them.

The sick woman, seeming totally dazed, stood facing towards me and I caught a glimpse of her face. It was red, but the grotesque swelling had completely disappeared. People rushed past me, stepping over the rope into the Spirit Circle, chattering, shouting and laughing. I fought my way back towards the woman, struggling for a second look at her face, but I could not get near her: crowds of people were hugging, touching and kissing her. Then someone lifted her up and she appeared high above the throng, lit by the flicker of fading firelight. There was no doubt that her face was healed. I was stunned. Never before had I witnessed such dramatic healing powers.

Rhythmic clapping and stamping thundered deafeningly around the Spirit Circle and my head reeled with power-plant fumes. I struggled towards the door, then I saw the sorcerer standing directly in front of me, the wolf's-head thrown back, his hair matted with sweat. He drank deeply from an ale pitcher, and behind him I saw baskets of cakes and trenchers of meat being piled near the fire. General revelry was taking over.

The sorcerer lowered the drinking vessel and looked directly at me, his eyes clear, bright and penetrating.

'Did you see it?' he shouted hoarsely above the din. 'Did you see the corn spirit?'

I did not know what to say. I could not say 'No', for I had just witnessed the most exhilarating event of my life. I had seen wonders I had not thought possible. I took the leather pitcher from the sorcerer, closed my eyes and swallowed the cool liquid. Then I passed the vessel back to him, cupped my hands around my mouth and shouted back:

'Yes. I saw!'

Dizzy and lightheaded, I stepped to the door and slipped out of the Spirit House into the chill dampness of the night. The midnight moon loomed majestically between towering clouds. Grey fire-smoke drifted and curled from the smoke-hole of the Spirit House, turning to silver in the moonlight; beneath the eaves, chinks of light flickered eerily in gaps around the door frame. Below, at the bottom of the hill, thatched roofs glistened with dew against the forest shadows and the very air seemed to shimmer with a spiritual force. I wandered slowly across the clearing, away from the noise of festivities filtering from the Spirit House, and found a seat at the edge of the forest astride the roots of an oak. The sights and sounds of the night's sorcery clamoured through my mind, and at the centre of it all images of the sorcerer chanting, singing, dancing and snarling beneath his wolf-skin. Excitedly, but carefully, I rehearsed in my mind all the details of the pagan ritual. When I had finished, I leaned back against the oak-trunk and spoke out loud the Lord's Prayer, looking up towards Heaven, far above the fading Saxon stars.

* * *

The night of the sorcerer's Spirit Circle is etched indelibly in my memory, for his healing power was an important thread in the web of events which led me inexorably into the world of Saxon sorcery. Only days before, I had landed on the Saxon shore as a servant of Almighty God, pledged to bring the light of our Saviour into the dark lands of the pagans. In His service, during that remarkable summer in the Year of Our Lord 674, I was to encounter soul-spirits and death demons, guardians and goddesses, and under the guidance of the Wolfman I was to learn the secrets of Saxon sorcery.

In the following pages I have recounted my experience as accurately as I can, for I believe that the lessons of the Wolfman are for people of all places and all times. In all humility, I dedicate this manuscript to spiritual seekers everywhere.

2

A FOREST OF PHANTOMS

THE DRAGON-PROWED wavecutter struck sail, drifted slowly through the morning mist and beached in a sheltered cove on the Saxon shore. Grey waves lapped at the stilled oars. I climbed stiffly into the chill water and stood, feet clamped by the cold, watching the boat and oarsmen slip silently out to sea, straining my eyes until the saffron sail melted into the mist. Then, scanning the beach anxiously, I waded ashore. There was no sign of the promised guide. I stood alone on the brink of the pagan wilderness.

Gulls wheeled warning of my presence and waves foamed on to the shingle with a sinister hiss. My eyes searched the cliff-tops uneasily as they loomed through floating fingers of mist; in my Mercian homeland the midwinter past had been marked by fire-balls in the sky and the peasants, seeing flying dragons spitting flame, had reverted in panic to the worship of devils and demons. Normally the stone boundaries of the Mercian monastery isolated me from such upheavals; the life of an apprentice scribe was almost totally contained within the cloisters. But now the events of midwinter seemed portentous indeed: with a party of monks I had journeyed south through the great forests to establish a mission at the court of the Saxon King. And now, in the warm, early days of summer, I stood deep in the pagan kingdom, sent from the mission to gather details of heathen customs and beliefs. I slipped a hand inside my tunic to finger again the bronze crucifix, hanging heavy and reassuring around my neck.

A curlew shrieked, invisible in the white cloaked sky and I was suddenly seized by the chilling conviction that I was being watched by some hidden figure or presence. Hurriedly I dried numbed feet on my woollen cloak and strapped on my shoes, fumbling to tie wet thongs under my knees. I picked my way over sour-smelling strands of kelpweed, crunched across a pebble beach into a marshy inlet and followed a meandering watercourse away from the beach into a ravine. Hills reached high into the sky and the landscape felt alien and strange. Beech trees stood huge and imposing, far taller than Mercian beeches, and strange blue and silver-spotted butterflies fluttered silently like coloured snowflakes. I saw birds that I did not recognise – small, streamlined and sharp-beaked. The beginnings of panic fluttered in my stomach and I bit my lower lip to control the attacks of anxiety. Gradually I was rewarded by a gathering crowd of comforting memories. I pictured the warm, tranquil afternoon of last spring, when Brother Eappa had appeared unexpectedly in the stone archway of my writing cell. He had padded to my table, arms straight down and still, hands clasped in front of him in his characteristic posture.

'Show me your work,' he had commanded. He was my teacher and had inspected my script many times. I turned the sheet of vellum towards him and he bent over, his tonsured head only inches from the page. After a long interval he had straightened up and I expected rebuke, for he seemed to be formulating his comments over-carefully in his mind.

His next words still echoed in my mind as if he had spoken them yesterday:

'Brand, I am soon to journey to the dark lands of the pagans. We are to establish a mission at the court of the Saxon King. You are to accompany me, for I shall need a scribe.'

I had stared at him in utter disbelief. Many missions left the monastery each summer, but I had never expected to be included in so holy an adventure. Indeed, I had never before travelled beyond the surrounding villages, let alone to another Kingdom. The prospect filled me with apprehension.

'But Brother Eappa, I am still young and have barely begun to know the glorious blessings of our Saviour. I am not yet a monk. There are many of the Brethren who are more worthy scribes than I.'

'There is much work best done by a young man, free from the monkly trappings of our Brothers,' he said, completely unmoved by my protest. Then he leaned down and spoke into my ear in a conspiratorial manner.

'The light of the Lord shines in your work, Brand. But I should like to see the love of God reach into your heart.' Eappa placed his hand on my head kindly. 'You have learned the scriptures well, you have learned to write well, you serve the Lord well with your mind. But after a mission in the wilderness of the pagans, you will love Him with all your heart.'

Eappa had said similar things to me before. I had protested that I did love God with all my heart, but I knew Eappa to be unconvinced. He seemed concerned that I should experience the Lord in a different way and I felt honoured that he should take such an interest in me.

Eventually the clouds lifted and on either side of the valley green hills materialised like colourful dream visions. Shouldering my bag, I left the stream bank and climbed the steep eastern slope which was smothered with white and pink pools of sweet-smelling yarrow flower. Walking, scrambling and finally climbing, I eventually reached the summit. It was a wonderful vantage point, lofty as an eagle's eyric. I surveyed the horizon in all directions. To the north, the hill on which I was standing formed a grassy spine stretching inland, broken only by coarse clumps of bramble. Below, to the south, white-capped waves swept into the rocks with a distant rumble, and to the west the stream snaked out of sight beyond the ravine. Carefully I scanned the beech forest to the east. The only sign of movement was a lone hawk, drifting in eerie silence through the sky, hunting prey far below in the forest glades. Sorting through my jumble of thoughts for a sensible strategy, I decided to sit on the hill facing the paths to the beach. If my guide approached the inlet he would have to walk along the hilltop or down the stream valley; either way I would have an early sight of him.

Distractedly I pulled barley bread from my bag, blessed it and washed it down with sweet red wine, musty from the leather flask. I remembered with pleasure the glow of pride in my father's eyes when I had told him of the proposed mission. My mother had said nothing, but hugged me until I thought I would burst. I recalled also the day of departure for the journey south, sharing tearful farewells with my parents, brothers and sisters; with a pang of guilt I remembered that while my heart had been sad, my stomach had bubbled with excitement and impatience to leave, although I had tried to hide my eagerness from my family. Sitting now amongst the daisies, on the hills of the heathens, I wondered whether Eappa had perhaps brought me on the mission with the express intention of sending me alone to meet the pagan guide, thus sparing his monks such dangers. Immediately I dismissed the dark thought from my mind. I needed determination, not doubts and suspicions.

My body still ached from the cramped boat journey and the warm sun had made me drowsy. I stretched out on my back and my ears sang with the hum of bees all around me in the cornflowers. I watched high, puffy clouds pouring gently like cream across the sky. Soon I sank into an exhausted sleep.

* * *

I awoke feeling chilled, sat bolt upright and with a start of alarm realised that I had slept well into the grey light of dusk. I climbed unsteadily to my feet and reeled with dizziness; the sleep had not refreshed me and I felt as unsteady as an ale-guzzler. I tried to focus my eyes on the approach paths to the beach. The sunset stained the sky blood-red and tips of the hills glowed green like a circle of giant burial mounds. Below, the valley lurked in darkness. Suddenly, out of the corner of my eye, I saw a flicker of movement in the shadows, barely a bow-shot downstream. Immediately I dropped to a crouch, my heart hammering against my chest, staring at the spot until my eyes flooded with tears; for the second time I was gripped by the conviction that I was being watched. Then, without warning, a stag bolted stiff-legged from the bushes and disappeared into the shadows. Rigid with fear, I clasped sweating palms together and chanted the Lord's Prayer over and over again, like an incantation. I had never experienced the Lord's presence, but I knew that He would protect me, for His Prayer drove terror from my mind.

After a time an early owl hooted in the forest below and thunderclouds rolled darkly across the sky. I decided to seek the shelter of the forest. Crossing myself, I rose quickly to my feet, scooped up my shoulder-bag and cloak and climbed down the hill, picking my steps carefully at first, then stumbling and sliding on my backside. Eventually I stepped through thinly spaced beeches which skirted the forest like silent sentries. Woodland shadows reached out to envelop me and it was too dark to follow animal paths; I had to work my way carefully through the trees, wading through thick undergrowth of golden fern and clinging brambles until, without warning, I emerged into a small clearing completely canopied by one gigantic beech tree. From the base of the beech two immense roots like dragon's claws rambled half-way across the open space. Working quickly in the gathering gloom, I heaped dry leaf-litter into the space between the roots to form a mattress. The shadows melted into darkness. Hurriedly I kicked aside the ground cover and dug a shallow fire-pit in the soft soil, cutting my fingers on invisible twigs as sharp as arrows. Then, piling tinder-dry kindling into the pit, I rummaged in my bag for the flint-and-iron. Blindly I struck them repeatedly in the darkness: eventually the sparks settled, crackled and grew into flames and I stoked the fire cautiously, nervous of dry vegetation under the beech canopy. I remembered building fires as a boy with my father, though it was always for a purpose: to warm the house, cook food, heat water or burn rubbish. I told myself now that the purpose of my fire was to frighten away wolves and bears, but in my heart I knew that it was to discourage the forces of terror that lurk in the night.

I settled back on to my mattress, leaf-litter crackling beneath me as I stared up into the tree. Bats glided silently between the beech branches, silhouetted momentarily against the grey night sky, and insects bustled noisily in my mattress. Many times as a boy I had slept under the stars, but now I lay on the floor of a heathen forest frozen by the fears of an alien traveller, my ears pricked for sounds of danger. My imagination lingered over tales told by travellers who had taken refuge in the monastery: stories of other travellers who had been attacked and robbed and of those who had lost their way and died of cold, hunger or wolves. Even worse, I was now becoming convinced that there would be no guide to accompany me through the pagan forest. I was sure that either I had been delivered to the cove on the wrong day or that the guide had been attacked and killed on his journey to meet me. I tried to control my panic. Carefully, methodically, I rehearsed in my mind the events leading up to my arrival on the lonely beach. The shadows had been lengthening on only the Mission's second day at the court of the pagan King when Eappa had decided to ask permission for me to travel through the kingdom, gathering information on the beliefs and superstitions of the heathens. No mission could begin work until it knew what errors were to be replaced by the light of the Lord and I was thrilled to learn that I was to be entrusted with such a vital task.

Eappa was confident that permission would be granted, for we were at the pagan court under the authority and protection of King Wulfhere, Christian ruler of all Mercia and the most powerful warlord in the land. Eappa went to the Royal Hall to seek an audience with the King, rejoining us shortly afterwards, as we sat on the grass inside the walled compound, to announce in his brisk manner that we were to see the King at sunset.

'Why doesn't he see us immediately?' snorted Brother Burghelm, his bald head trembling with indignation. 'Surely he will refuse permission? He only barely tolerates our presence as it is and is under no obligation to aid our Mission.'

'Are you sure this is the right time for such a request?' Brother Padda whined. 'This worshipper of devils has shown us no charity since we left the shadow of Wulfhere's kingdom. Why should he do so now? He will probably allow Brand to travel into the forest and then have him killed, pleading with Wulfhere that it was the work of robbers.'

Padda's doubts chilled me to the marrow.

'Are you all growing cold with fear?' Eappa hissed contemptuously, staring at us one by one. We all dropped our heads in shame.

'If Brand is allowed to journey he will need no protection, for the Lord God Almighty will accompany him.'

I swallowed hard and wished that my faith were as strong as Eappa's.

'The pagan will grant what we ask, for fear of Wulfhere's wrath,' he continued. 'And if the King lets Brand travel in the heathen lands then, with the information he gathers, the Lord will deliver the Saxons into our hands.'

We made the short walk to the Royal Hall shortly before sunset. The King listened in stony silence to Eappa's request, staring at each of us in turn with eyes like ice.

When Eappa had finished a bent old man, sitting on a stool next to the King, struggled to his feet. He cupped his hand and twittered like a bird into the King's ear. I could not hear what he said, but I saw the King's face crease into a broad smile and he nodded slowly, evidently pleased with what he had heard.

'You wish the scribe to travel unhindered, to witness the ways and gods of my people? Permission is granted. And I shall provide a guide.'

The beech branches groaned in the night wind, moving ponderously like giant hands high above my head; for a moment I was dragged back into the present. It was clear now that there would be no guide and that I had been abandoned, without a map or directions. Tears stung my cheeks and I took the crucifix from inside my tunic, held it on my chest and virtually willed memories of the monastery to visit me like old friends. Closing my eyes, I recalled the faces and voices of the intitiates with whom I lived, and the sound of their laughter at private jokes shared out of earshot of the monks. I loved the regular routine: ringing bells in the night to pluck us from our dormitory beds, sleepy matins sung with the brethren, the six o'clock service, the seven psalms with the litanies and the chapter Eucharist. Then eagerly to breakfast; the memory of it awakened hunger pangs in my stomach. Without opening my eyes, I felt around inside my bag for barley bread and chewed on it slowly.

Work in the scriptorium followed breakfast, with the smell of parchment and the scratching of quills like a dawn chorus of strange birds. This was my favourite time of the day, for among the initiates I was Eappa's most prized scribe. I served the Almighty well with my quill.

Soon I slipped into troubled slumber. I do not know how long I slept before I began to dream, but the images of that night were to live with me for ever. I dreamed that a warm wind was sweeping into my face, tugging at my hair and tunic. I struggled to open my eyes and my vision cleared. I was speeding over open meadows, travelling at least twenty feet above ground and when I approached dense woodland I rose much higher, skimming above the tops of the trees. The sensation of flying was exhilarating. Soon the air became cool and moist and in the distance, against the dawn sky, I saw a rapidly approaching shoreline. Gathering speed, I shot over the beach and out to sea, rocking and plunging across the waves as if I were riding in some invisible boat.

Eventually I approached another coastline, shrouded in mist, the bare outlines of a beach gleaming wetly, bounded by a low cliff promontory topped with heavy tree-cover. I moved to within hailing distance of the shoreline, then wallowed gently above the shadows. I scanned the entire beach area, but could see no movement or activity and all seemed deserted. Then I was steered towards the open beach, skimmed to a landing and found myself sitting on sand and shells, in a few inches of water. The sand inclined gradually from the water to a ridge or rock, covered by trees and scrub, the ridge marking the back boundary of the beach.

I paddled out of the water, on to the sand and looked back up and down the beach. There was no sign of people, nor anything to indicate why I had been brought to this particular place. The only sounds were the cawing of seabirds and the slap of water on shingles.

I walked up the beach towards the ridge, scrambled up the rock and heaved myself on to the ridge top. The ground was covered with dense brambles and beyond that a thick forest of oak, gnarled and old. I knew that I was to walk into the oaks, for there was something waiting for me behind the trees. I pushed through the scrub into the tree cover and, almost immediately, entered a small clearing. To my astonishment there stood, in the centre of the clearing, an enormous stake, thick and tall as a tree, but smooth-sided. The stake was covered with carved symbols running vertically up the sides and I recognised some of them as runes, the mysterious writing of the pagans. My eyes followed the carvings to the top of the stake, and then froze in horror, for at the top sat a black horse-head, sightless eyes staring down, nostrils flaring and mouth gaping horribly. I was terrified. I wanted to run, but my body was paralysed, rooted to the patch of God-forsaken ground.

Summoning forth all my will, I forced a scream from my lips

and immediately my body came to life. I scrambled backwards, out of the clearing, leaped from the ridge to the beach below and sprinted towards the water. Sand and shells shifted under my feet and I felt as if I was hardly moving. Each time I drove down with my right foot, a sharp pain shot through my shinbone; the jump had twisted my ankle. It took an age to reach the water but at last, with a supreme effort, I plunged desperately into the sea. Before I could even begin to swim, I was swept away from the shore by the invisible force that had borne me here in the first place. Drenched and gasping for breath, I turned to look back at the beach. Above the treeline on the rocky ridge peered the dreaded horse's head, the eye-hollows seeming to stare directly at me. Suddenly a massive black shadow burst from the head and plunged over the water towards me. The wind tore a scream from my lips as I shot over the water parallel with the shore and then sped out into the open sea.

I kept my eyes shut all the way back until I began to bump and roll over the land, careening over meadows and forest, and had to fling out my arms to maintain my balance.

I awoke flailing about on my leafy mattress, muttering and groaning out loud. I lay still, sweat beading my forehead as I tried to get my bearings. The moon had slunk behind clouds, pitching the forest into darkness. From a distance wolf howls split the night air and echoed mournfully through the tree-tops. I lay still as a gravestone while the forest fell eerily, ominously silent. Then, almost imperceptibly at first, the whole forest began to tremble. I lifted my head and stared blindly into the surrounding blackness, beyond the fading embers of the fire. I could see nothing. A rumbling noise grew rapidly louder and louder, like thunder, until the forest shadows rocked and swayed and I thought the trees would come crashing to the ground. I lurched to my feet and my crucifix slipped from my chest; frantically I scrabbled in the leaf litter until I found it and then slumped against the tree trunk, my shouted prayers snatched away by the uproar. Giant black clouds still blotted out the moon and in the darkness the air around me seemed crowded with spectres, invisible tormenters hissing from tree to tree, shrieking in front and then behind me so that I did not know in which direction to turn. Then, crashing into the clearing came a pack of monstrous black dogs, pounding past me with a horrible, rasping howl, and on their heels thundered a herd of enormous horses, black as night, with the same hideous, staring eyes as the horse-head of my nightmare. Astride the leading horse rode a shadowy figure, cape flooding out behind him like the wings of a demon, bearing straight down on me. At the last moment the horse veered to my left and charged past, followed by twenty or more horses and riders, kicking up the embers of my fire into the black night air.

The din died away as abruptly as it had arisen. Leaves swirled silently to the ground through air thick with dust and I sank to my knees, clutching my crucifix in trembling hands. Never had I suffered such a terrifying ordeal, not even in my wildest imaginings. Kneeling alone in the forest, I prayed again for my salvation and for deliverance from the monstrous beings.

*　*　*

The night dragged on, slow and menacing as a black adder. I lay in shocked stillness for I know not how long, huddled at the base of the beech, not daring to move yet dreading the return of the spectres.

Eventually I lifted my head and peered around, hardly breathing. I could see nothing in the blackness and cursed the moon for deserting me. Darkness had held especial fears for me ever since childhood nightmares had haunted my sleep: dreams of wolves and birds of prey, hunting me like an animal. But none were as bad as the nightmare I had suffered this night.

Taut as a bowstring, I crept cautiously into the clearing, fumbling in the darkness for dry kindling. Suddenly struck cold by the thought that my fire might have attracted the monsters in the first place, I immediately abandoned my plan and returned to the refuge of the beech.

I tried to unravel my tormented and tangled thoughts. For a while I thought that, if I survived the night, I would return to the seashore in the hope of attracting the attention of a trading ship. But I did not cling to the idea for long, because I knew that it was ridiculous; even a coast-hugging Saxon vessel would be unlikely to venture into a deserted cove. I had no choice but to head inland, where I would surely encounter a settlement or at least a farm. Perhaps from there I could obtain a guide to take me to a landing harbour where I might gain passage away from this land.

After what seemed an age, moonlight filtered through the branches, picking out flowering shrubbery like silver filigree. Taking comfort in the soft light, I began to think of Eappa and the Mission. I thought about the reasons they had sent me into the forest and the importance to the Mission of any information I could gather. I thought of the trust Eappa had placed in me and I began to feel ashamed of my fears. I had only suffered a nightmare and Eappa had taught me that such things were merely the ravings of a tormented mind. And the creatures which had stampeded through the clearing, be they spectres or remnants of my nightmare, had not hurt me.

I recalled stories told to us by Eappa about the true men of God, who braved ordeals for the glory of the Lord. I thought of Guthlac, most revered of missionaries, who had been attacked by demons in the wastelands of the East Angles and had repelled the monsters with the power of prayer. Indeed, there were many virtuous hermits, servants of the Lord who – for the name of God – longed for the wilderness and lived there. These hermits lived in lands which men would not occupy because of the accursed spirits which infested such wastelands. Sometimes, Eappa said, these men of our Lord were visited in the quiet of the night by great multitudes of such devils. They were terrible in appearance: they had huge heads, long necks and scraggy faces, with shaggy ears, crooked noses, cruel eyes and foul mouths. Eappa said their teeth were like wolf fangs and their throats filled with flame.

I remembered the tale of one holy hermit who, in the night, suddenly heard the bellowing of various wild beasts and shortly afterwards saw the shapes of all manner of creatures coming towards him, and could hear the howling of wolves, croaking of ravens and grunting of pigs all around him. The servant of our Lord armed himself with the weapon of Christ's crucifix and, clasping it in his hand, he scorned the threats of the demons, shouting at them; immediately all the accursed spirits had fled away.

The words he had used, taught to us by Eappa, rang clearly in my memory: 'Oh you wretched, perverse spirits, your power is seen and your might is made known. Now, wretches, you take on the form of wild beasts, and birds and serpents, you who formerly exalted yourselves when you aspired to be equal to God. Now I command you in the name of the eternal Lord, who made you and flung you from the height of Heaven, to cease from this disturbance!'

I heard my voice ringing around the clearing and I realised that I had been shouting the prayer with all my might. I sat still and listened but there was no sound save for the distant hooting of an owl. I felt stronger and an anger began to well up inside me. I glared into the looming forest and defiantly hurled another prayer against the phantoms, figments of my nightmare: 'Woe to you, children of darkness. You are dust and ashes and cinders. I am here and ready and await the will of my Lord; why should you frighten me with your false threats?' The forest shadows shrank back and the moon seemed to beam approvingly. I reached inside my tunic and slipped the crucifix around my neck. It was heavy and solid and I knew it would keep me safe from pagan demons, just as it had more worthy servants than I.

Determinedly, I buckled on my cloak, looped the bag over my shoulder and turned to walk from the clearing to pursue my Mission.

As soon as I took a step, however, I cried out in pain. With a sense of dread I recalled my damaged ankle, injured in my flight from the nightmare horse-head demon. The phantoms crept back around me like a cold, clammy mist and what I had dismissed as a dream now prowled through the night, seething with the danger of daytime demons. But I had made up my mind. The Lord had sustained me so far and would protect me again. Setting my face towards the hills, I took a deep breath and walked slowly into the mist.

3

TALES OF PAGAN POWERS

I HOBBLED out of the forest and back up the hillside. At the summit I collapsed, nursing my ankle until the pain eased. To the west, across the moonlit landscape, the ravine lay in darkness; on the eastern horizon, thunderclouds rolled through the grey sky like raiding ships sneaking silently up on the moon.

Eventually I got to my feet and trudged northward along the hilltop, accompanied only by the soft hiss of the wind. Suddenly I stopped, staring intently into the distance: a long bow-shot ahead, against a boulder bordering the track, slumped the figure of a man who was apparently sleeping. Immediately I suspected an ambush and dropped to a crouch, anxiously scanning the shrubbery on either side of the track for a hidden accomplice. But the vegetation consisted of grass and low scrub; apart from the rock there was nowhere a robber could hide. Just then, without warning, a cloud sailed across the moon and the figure disappeared into shadow. I peered intently at the boulder — thinking, hoping, that the man was a figment of my imagination — but when the moon re-emerged, he was still sitting motionless against the rock.

I considered skirting the area by creeping down the hill, along the perimeter of the woods and rejoining the path well beyond the sleeping figure. But weariness gave me courage and I now felt certain that I had to contend with one man only. I unstrapped my knife and drew it from the belt-sheath; it felt heavy and cumbersome. Transferring it to my right hand, I crept cautiously to within ten paces of the motionless figure, hoping to slip by without waking him.

Then my heart stopped for the man looked up slowly, as if he had been aware of my presence all along, his face hidden in moon-shadow cast by a floppy, wide-brimmed hat.

He rose smoothly to his feet and glided towards me, walking with a cat-like lightness and balance. I tightened my grip on the knife, but he stopped a few paces away from me, tipped back his hat and looked at me quizzically.

'May I ask who you are, walking by moonlight over the graves of giants?'

His voice, heavy with Saxon dialect, hung in the night air.

'I am Wat Brand, freeman of Mercia,' I answered, as boldly as I could manage. 'I am journeying in these lands under the protection of your King.'

With a dramatic flourish the stranger swept off his hat and bowed deeply; for a moment I thought he was mocking me, but then he straightened up and smiled broadly.

'I am called Wulf. I am your guide. May I be of service?'

I stared at him in astonishment.

'Are you the guide appointed by the King?' I asked, incredulous.

'The King requested my services,' he replied and proffered his hand in greeting; hurriedly I sheathed my knife and gripped his hand in response. He looked directly into my eyes with a gaze remarkably penetrating, yet open and friendly. Indeed, his whole appearance was very striking. In the moonlight his beard and shoulder-length hair glowed gold above the clothes of a traveller: long, faded blue cloak, light-coloured tunic and leggings and strong boots laced to the calves. His face, dominated by large, wide-set eyes and strong nose, was given a strangely melancholy expression by long, sloping eyebrows.

'Why are you travelling by night?' he asked pointedly. 'Why not rest until daybreak?'

'Why were you not on the beach to meet me?' I retorted defensively. I did not wish to describe my forest nightmare, for I felt such a story would sound absurd.

'My apologies,' he said immediately, apparently contrite. 'I had business elsewhere and was delayed.'

He was watching me very closely and I had the uneasy feeling that he was looking for tell-tale signs of my ordeal.

'There is no point in journeying further tonight, now that we have met. Let us rest together under the trees,' he said, smiling disarmingly.

Reluctantly I nodded my acquiescence, anxious to conceal my fear of the forest.

Wulf collected his bag and strode fleet-footed down the hill, his cloak flapping around him like a raven's wings. I scrambled after him, wincing with pain from the ankle and feeling the grip of fear tighten around my throat as we padded into the dark confines of the forest. Barely a hundred paces into the shadows, Wulf stopped in a small clearing crushed from the undergrowth by a fallen oak, lying huge and moss-covered like a toppled, long-dead giant.

'Rest yourself,' he said, sweeping off his hat again and gesturing towards the tree as if he were greeting me as a guest in his house.

Watching him warily, I stepped over the branches and sat with my back against a clear area of trunk while my guide bustled around, collecting kindling and piling it in the middle of the clearing. I noticed that the ground was black from previous fires; obviously Wulf was already familiar with this area of the forest.

He hunched over the kindling, sparked flame from flint and iron and expertly coaxed the fire to a full blaze. Then he sat next to me, so close that we were almost touching, and warmed his hands by the flames.

'You must be important,' he said airily. 'I was engaged to guide you by a messenger of the King. Are you royal-born?'

My mind was racing, for I had never before encountered a stranger in such alien surroundings. This question puzzled me, for I had already told him that I was a freeman and not royal. I decided to admit as little as possible; it might suit my purpose to disguise the true nature of my mission.

'What did they tell you?' I asked guardedly.

Wulf tipped his hat to the back of his head and leaned forward towards the hissing fire.

'They told me that you are to be guided to our gods,' he replied, maintaining his pleasant manner. 'Why does the King wish you to know the powers of the Mighty Ones?'

'Your King would like knowledge of your gods spread to other kingdoms; I am to take back the teachings of your priests to my homeland.'

The lie was cast before I knew what I was saying, but it sounded convincing and I was pleased with it. Wulf turned his head slowly and looked me full in the face, his eyes cold and shiny as hoarfrost.

'You serve the priests of the new god,' he said softly. 'Tell me how you come to prowl in our forests, carrying your god like a concealed dagger?'

I was stunned by his sudden change in mood and his knowledge of my mission. Nervously I eyed the heavy knife strapped to his belt-sheath. He looked strong and experienced and I knew I would stand no chance in a fight. I started talking feverishly, anxious to placate him.

'The Mercian King is powerful. So powerful that all the rulers of southern kingdoms pay him homage. In the first warm days of spring he commanded Aethelwealh, ruler of your kingdom, to attend the Mercian royal court. There Aethelwealh was ordered to take as his Queen the Christian princess Eabe of the Hwicce people. And on the wedding day Aethelwealh and his court were baptised into the faith of the Lord.'

I paused, avoiding Wulf's probing stare and running an agitated hand over my close-cropped head.

'Aethelwealh submitted to such a humiliation?' he said, sounding more curious than shocked.

'Aethelwealh dared not refuse the arrangement,' I replied. Wulf raised his eyebrows in surprise and I did not mention that the Mercian King had sweetened the pagan ruler by granting him additional lands on the south coast. 'When your King prepared to return to these lands, the Mercian monarch commanded that he bring with him a small party of monks to attend to the spiritual needs of Queen Eabe. But he also ordered that your King should cooperate with the monks in creating a Mission for Our Lord the Saviour among your people. I am a scribe and serve Brother Eappa, leader of the Mission.'

Wulf pursed his lips and whistled softly, apparently impressed. Relating the powerful royal authority for my presence seemed to have won respect from my guide and my embarrassment in being caught in a lie melted in a sudden flush of confidence. I allowed myself a smug smile.

Wulf tugged at his beard thoughtfully. 'What do you wish to know of our gods?' he asked, sounding as friendly as when I had encountered him on the hilltop.

'Everything,' I asserted boldly. 'The very nature of your beliefs; the names of the gods, the dates and purposes of your festivals and the powers of your priests.'

I had been instructed to take particular interest in the priests of paganism, for it was these people whom the mission would seek to replace with servants of the Lord.

Wulf covered his mouth with his hand. For an instant I thought that he was hiding a sly smile, but when he dropped his hand his expression was serious.

'We are simple people, with simple beliefs. We worship the sun, the moon and the stars on account of their shining brightness. We believe in fire because of its sudden heat; also water and the earth because they nourish all things.' He shrugged his shoulders dismissively. 'That is the extent of it. Your task should be easily accomplished – there is really nothing more to know.'

Wulf squatted in front of the fire, poking the embers with an oak stick and sending showers of sparks shooting into the night air. The conversation seemed to be over as far as he was concerned and I did not know what to say; indeed, I felt embarrassed for him. His beliefs were as manifestly in error as the monks had forewarned, for the South Saxons had yet to learn that He is the true God who created the sun, moon, stars and earth for the enjoyment and use of man. These things were not to be worshipped as gods.

Wulf leaned back against the oak trunk and looked at me sideways. 'Your god must be very powerful,' he said, his manner betraying a hint of awe.

'He is. He is the Creator of everything. And now in the kingdom of Mercia, crimes and outrages against the property of the church are punished with a fine as heavy as that for treason against the King himself.'

Again I had the uneasy feeling that Wulf was chuckling to

himself, but if there was a smile on his lips it disappeared instantly.

'Our gods are not worth discussing. They are fools – like the spoiled children of a petty king,' he said.

I looked at him in astonishment and thought his gods must indeed be weak and worthless, for similar blasphemies against the Lord Almighty would surely result in eternal damnation. If the South Saxons spoke so disparagingly of all their gods, then the mission to preach the word of God would meet little difficulty.

'Can you really denigrate your gods with impunity?' I asked, my confidence fuelled now by a sense of superiority.

Just then a clap of thunder rumbled in the distance and I sat upright in alarm. Wulf began chuckling as if at some private joke.

'See!' he said, pointing towards the sky. 'Old Thunor, the Thunderer, is taking offence. I suspected that he was eavesdropping. Now what kind of god worth his wergild fines would concern himself with remarks passed in conversation by mere mortals like us?'

I looked nervously at the night sky, grey and flat above the treetops, listening keenly for more thunder. The sound was terrifying, reminiscent of the rumble preceding my nightmare encounter with the forest hunters.

'Let me tell you a story about the Thunderer,' Wulf continued loudly, frowning melodramatically and glaring in mock abuse towards the sky. 'It will prove to you what a fool he is. One time he was travelling in the land of the giants, when he came upon the mead hall of the mightiest giant of all and knocked on the door to ask for hospitality.'

Wulf leapt to his feet and stood with legs spread wide apart, banging his fist on an imaginary door. Then he jumped on to the oak trunk and bellowed the giant's response. ' "I admit to my hall only those who are masters of some trial. What can a puny individual like you hope to achieve against my giant warriors?" '

Dropping to the ground, Wulf voiced the Thunderer's challenge: 'There is no one here can eat faster than I.' Then he sat on the log and continued his narrative excitedly. 'An enormous trencher was brought in. Thunor sat down at one end and a giant warrior at the other, and they both ate as fast as they could. They met in the middle of the trencher and Thunor thought he had at least matched the giant for speed of eating. But then he saw that while he had left only the bones of his meat, the giant had eaten all his meat, bones and the trencher as well. Thunor had lost the contest.'

Wulf collapsed in a fit of mirth, and was so overcome that he had to rest a hand on my shoulder for support until he had regained his composure. I was so transfixed by his total, animated involvement in his story and his sudden change of mood that I was taken completely by surprise when another crash of thunder rocked the night sky, sending me leaping to my feet with a shout.

'But wait!' Wulf said, pulling me back to the ground. 'There is more. Thunor was too stupid to be dismayed by this defeat. He challenged all the giants in the mighty mead hall to a drinking contest. The giants produced an enormous ale-horn, and challenged the Thunderer to empty it.'

Wulf's eyes popped as he enacted Thunor's attempt to empty the imaginary horn; I sat frozen with fear, watching the midnight charade and listening for the threatening, deep-throated boom of thunder. Sitting on the log, Wulf plunged back into the narrative.

'Thunor took three immense draughts, but was unable to empty the horn. At this the giants roared with laughter, and the mightiest giant said, "This mockery has lasted long enough; after all, Thunor is a mere weakling compared with such mighty beings as we have here." '

Wulf leapt to his feet again, standing astride in his Thunderer characterisation, his eyes blazing. I glanced nervously at the sky; purple thunderclouds rolled across the face of the moon and in the firelight Wulf's animated body projected huge shadows against the silent trees.

'Thunderer was now furious. He shouted, "Now I am really angry and I will show you how strong I am. I challenge any of you giants to a wrestling match." The giants laughed and beckoned into the hall a bent old crone, shuffling forward to take up his challenge. And although Thunor tried with all his strength, he could struggle only evenly with the old woman and eventually she threw him to the ground." '

Wulf's shoulders heaved with laughter. This seemed to be the end of his tale.

'Is that the point of the story?' I asked. 'Your god was totally humiliated by the giants?'

'He was,' Wulf nodded, his words swallowed by chuckles. 'He turned to leave the hall, his head hung in shame. But then the Mighty Giant called him back, and said, "Had I known you were so powerful I would never have admitted you to my hall, for I would have been afraid of you." '

Wulf paused dramatically, his eyes twinkling, stroking his moustache as if wiping away the smiles.

'But how so, Wulf? Surely he had lost every contest?'

'Yes, but the Giant then revealed that Thunderer's opponents had not been as they had appeared. Thunor had in fact competed for speed of eating with Wildfire itself, which can consume entire forests at one sitting. And the enormous drinking horn had been connected to the oceans, and in each of his three draughts Thunor had succeeded in lowering the level of the sea by one inch.'

I laughed with him. 'But what about the old woman who wrestled him to the ground?'

'The crone was Thunderer's most formidable opponent, for she who finally threw him to the ground was Old Age itself.'

Wulf cackled happily and crouched in front of the fire, lightly smothering the flames with wood ash and piling more wood carefully on top to ensure a slow burn that would last the night. I sat looking in wonder at my strange guide and thinking about his story. Begun as a jest at the expense of his Thunder god, it had ended by portraying him as powerful indeed, a being who could challenge the very forces of nature. But if Wulf had related the story to impress me with the might of his gods he had failed, for the Thunderer was not in command of those forces he had challenged. I felt secure in the knowledge that our Lord and Saviour was all-powerful, the true Creator and ruler of all forces.

I glanced up above the trees and gasped in amazement; the thunderclouds were dispersing like smoke in the wind and within a few moments they had pulled away to leave vast areas of clear sky. I was still trying to absorb the astonishing phenomenon when Wulf turned back towards me.

'Now, the giants are very different,' Wulf enthused, settling back against the log and brushing fire ash from his tunic. 'The giants tower far above human size. They stand like mighty oaks, rooted to the ground but with their heads in the clouds. Usually they are as good-natured as lambs, but if they are provoked they can be very dangerous. When their wrath is kindled they rage and thunder, uproot trees and hurl rocks, squeeze water out of stones. And in temper they stamp on the ground with such force that their legs are buried up to the knees.'

He roared with laughter again, thumping his right foot on the ground in imitation of the giants. I chuckled at the prodigious deeds of strength he claimed for them, but listened warily for the point of the story. I thought he might try to turn a tale against the Lord Almighty, since he had already laughed at his own god.

'I will tell you how big they are,' he chuckled, leaning forward dramatically with his eyes brimming with mirth. 'One day a giant had got something in his eye that pricked him; it was making his eye water. He tried to get it out with his finger, but that was too bulky. So he took a sheaf of corn and with that he managed to remove the speck in his eye. Then he picked it up and examined it on the end of his finger. "Why, it's a fir-cone!" he said. "Who would have thought a little thing like that could have hurt me so?" '

We both laughed uproariously. The giants had taken on a sense of the ridiculous. Wulf continued his narrative in a sing-song voice as if he were talking to a child.

'Once there was a giant maiden. As she was walking in enormous bounds across the hills, she looked down and saw something moving. Bending to her knees, she picked up a ploughman with his horse and plough. Putting them on her lap, she watched with curiosity as they crawled and slipped about in panic. Finally she carried them to her mother and asked, "What kind of beetle can this be, mother, that I have found rooting up the ground in tiny furrows?" '

I laughed out loud, but Wulf was not amused. He waited for me to quieten down, then continued: 'So the mother looked at the creatures crawling on her daughter's palm. "Put them away, child," she said. "We have to leave this land soon, and they are to live here instead." '

Wulf reported the mother's reply in a tone of great sadness, his mood changing with startling suddenness. He sat in silence, his face mournful.

'Wulf, would you prefer that the giants still ruled over these lands?' I asked at last, unable to stand the uneasy silence.

'They will again,' he said, spreading his arms, hands open towards the sky. 'That is the way of wyrd. Events flow in cycles like the tides of the ocean. The same thing will happen to us one day.'

I stared at him in disbelief.

'Eventually people will have to make way for the tiny creatures that crawl about in our mattresses,' he went on. 'Then we shall be the lumbering outcasts, slipping ever further towards exile.'

I bit back a retort. It was surely not the prerogative of man to pronounce on the future. And all creatures were put into the world by God to serve man, even if we did not understand how they were meant to serve us.

'The giants are the gods of old,' he said in a low voice. 'The world was made from giants, in the first winter. A mighty giant was created from hoarfrost. And when fire came, he melted. From the enormous bulk of his body came the worlds. From his blood flowed the sea, from his bones the mountains, from his hair the forests, from his skull the sky. And from his lashes, covering the eyes that beheld all, was fashioned Middle-Earth, land of people, sorcerers and spirits. In the centre of Middle-Earth, on hills rising high as mountains, live the gods, and below seethes the Underworld, land of the dead and all their secrets.'

Wulf looked up towards the night sky, his eyes hooded, concealing his emotion from me. 'The giants are now outcasts, living as exiles on the fringe of the earth, kept at bay by a mighty ocean surrounding Middle-Earth.'

He fell silent again. I wanted to ask him more, for he was telling me exactly what I had been sent to hear. But he seemed deeply affected by his story and sat staring at the grey wisps of smoke climbing from the fire into the night sky. I felt embarrassed for him. His obvious sincerity diluted slightly the revulsion I felt for his erroneous story of the Creation, but almost certainly he had not intended to open his heart so readily to a stranger.

'We are taught a truth very different from the story you have told me,' I said at last, hoping to draw him out of his sadness and back into conversation. 'I cannot imagine ever encountering your gods.'

Wulf turned to look directly at me, his eyes twinkling brightly through the gloom.

'You already have,' he replied, in a voice strangely flat and toneless.

I frowned in puzzlement.

'This very night,' he prompted, raising an eyebrow knowingly.

The terror of the horse-head dream and the huntsmen flooded back into my body and my whole world fell in. Wulf's knowledge of my ordeal in the forest spun me into confusion and I suddenly felt totally unprotected and vulnerable, as if he could read my thoughts and know my deepest secrets.

Wulf leaned forward, his eyes never leaving mine, his face crinkling into a smile. He spoke in a whisper.

'I know, because my reality is the sorcerer's reality. I can enter the world of spirits and they showed me what happened to you as clearly as if I were watching images moving in a still pool.'

Dumbfounded and frightened, I desperately wanted to fill the silence with a statement, reply, question: anything. But I could say nothing.

'The spirits of death acknowledged you,' he said with conviction. 'If Woden had not swept his huntsmen over your forest camp, then I would not – indeed *could* not – have served as your guide. I waited on the hilltop until Woden marked you out.'

He jumped up and paced energetically around the fire. All melancholy thoughts of the giants seemed to have left him.

'Woden is greybeard among our gods,' he continued animatedly. 'He is god of the magic song, incantations, words of power. For nine nights Woden hung on the Tree of Knowledge, swept by the wind of destiny. He was pierced by the spears of Knowledge but he did not bleed. He hung there without food or drink; he hung there in a fast until he was transported to the mountain of the gods. There he was shown the secrets of the runes and the incantations that unravel the secrets of Middle-Earth.

'This is why Woden had to mark you out. Only he chooses who may be guided to the secrets.'

Wulf stopped pacing and stood facing me, feet astride, thumbs hooked into his woven leather belt, casting his face in dramatic, moving shadows.

'Brand, when Woden marked you out I knew that I could guide you. You have been granted access to the spirits.'

I stared at his face in the moving fire shadows, looking desperately for clues, signs, reassurance – I knew not what.

'The spirits?' My voice sounded tiny and cracked and I coughed to camouflage it. Wulf looked at me from under half-closed lids – a devastating look, full of craft and cunning.

'The spirits are the custodians of our knowledge. If you wish me to guide you to our gods, then I can show you secrets your masters never dreamed of. But I warn you: the secrets of the spirits cannot be encompassed by words passed between us. You must encounter the spirits directly.'

I was still stunned by Wulf's knowledge of my ordeal with the spectral huntsmen, but talk of spirits served only to compound my terror. I had survived the spectres in the forest, with the help of God Almighty, but to purposely seek them out smacked of evil. Spirits were devils, agents of evil, to be dismissed from the minds of pagans and supplanted by the Seed of Truth, the Word of God. Indeed, Eappa had warned me that pagan sorcerers steal the souls of the peasants through pacts with the devils. What Eappa had not told me – what he could not know – was that my guide was a sorcerer.

Wulf scrutinised me steadily as my thoughts whirled and spun.

'Wulf, couldn't you just *tell* me about the spirits? All I wish to know are the names of your gods and the nature of your beliefs, and perhaps to observe your people at their worship.'

Wulf strolled back towards the fallen oak.

'If you do not wish to be guided by me, then I shall take you to a trading harbour tomorrow and you can leave. Let me know your decision in the morning.'

He wrapped himself in his cloak, lay down and closed his eyes, seeming to fall asleep instantly. I watched him closely for a moment, but he did not stir. The conversation was over.

A piece of wood shifted in the fire. I watched it fall slowly, eaten away in mouthfuls by the flames. My mind was racing, bursting with ideas, voices, questions, warnings. For the second time that night I contemplated going to a harbour and obtaining passage back along the coast to the Royal Hall and the friendly faces of the Mission. But now Eappa's voice haunted me: 'We cannot deliver the pagan from the forces of evil until we know the nature of his errors.' If the secrets of pagan power lay in the devils, then surely I should, in Wulf's words, 'encounter them directly'. Yet I was sure that Eappa never expected or intended me to venture so far into the dark world of pagan sorcery, for he preached that such things were the province of devils. He had instructed me to travel, observe, listen and remember. But he had never suggested that I *enter* the world of devils.

I sighed and leaned back on the mossy oak trunk. My eyes were heavy, my mind exhausted, but I was too scared to go to sleep. My thoughts wandered. Absently, I imagined myself returning to the Mission to tell unheard-of secrets about the pagans, astounding the monks with my knowledge and graciously accepting Eappa's praise for my courage. Smiling, I pulled my cloak more closely around my shoulders. Gradually my eyes tired of watching the dancing fire and my lids sank shut. Slumber sneaked up on me and stole my thoughts. I dropped into a deep and vivid dream. I was back in the monastery, lying on the hard oak bed relieved by only the thinnest of mattresses. The echo of bolts sounded down the corridors long and bare, as the sub-prior locked the cloister doors. The heavy reek of oil, which had been burning with floating wicks in stone cressets, filled my nostrils with that surge of familiarity so often carried by forgotten smells. The other boys in the dormitory were fast asleep, curled into shadowy lumps in rows of beds stretching into the darkness on either side of me.

Then, almost immediately, I heard the bells ringing to awaken us before dawn and the sub-prior was touring the dormitory with lighted lantern to see that no one had overslept. Huddled together like lambs for warmth, we shuffled in a line out of the dormitory towards the chapel, hard cold floors slapping and clapping under our sandals. On my right I saw a stone archway leading to a workroom still dank with darkness. I knew that inside, displayed in various stages of preparation, lay strips of calfskin which would become fine and glorious bookcovers. Just past this room lay the steps leading to the cellarer's vault, packed neatly with supplies, implements, food, clothes and blankets, tallow for dormitory candles and beeswax for altar candles.

The entrance to the chapel was thronged with monks cloaked in pre-dawn silence; mostly men of thane class, high wergild-holders turned from battle pledges to prayer. Beyond them, hung on chains at the door, glowed red coals in black iron dishes to warm the hands of those who were to minister at the altar. Everything seemed so familiar, even the little clouds of cold breath puffing out from people's faces and the sleepy but friendly eyes – a warm bond of brotherhood, wrapped around us all.

Then something strange happened. Everyone stood aside, gowns stiff with cold rustling as the monks melted back into the darkness. I passed into the chapel alone. The small room was exactly as it had always been: wall-hung with tapestries depicting angels picked out in weft-threads, softly lit by candles in finely enamelled hanging bowls. In the centre was the altar, decorated with fine pieces of silver lovingly polished and lit by tall altar candles.

I moved towards the altar, but stopped suddenly, gripped by horror. On tables and shelves behind sat literally dozens of strangely carved icons, many encrusted with gold and precious stones which glowed in the light of the candles. Some were small and squat, others larger than men, but all were grotesquely covered with strange inscriptions. I moved around the room, powerless to stop myself, as if on a guided tour of hell; animal motifs and heathen designs loomed from the walls, and large figures with human heads and smooth, sightless eyes. I was alone in the hideous room, too frightened even to cry out, paralysed by the cold and eerie presence. Desperately I looked towards the altar again and there, crowded on to a platform alone with piles of icons, rested a simple golden cross. I dropped to my knees and prayed fervently, snatches of prayers from every kind of service and lesson, anything that would restore the warm, protective mantle of God.

Then I heard movement. I opened my eyes and, through tears of fear and emotion, I saw the figure of a man. At first I thought it was Eappa, but then I realised that his face was different. Kindness, warmth, love and caring poured from him like a warm summer wind. I blinked my eyes clear and looked again; now he appeared strangely like Wulf, but disguised by a cowl. He opened a thick Mass book, fine vellum leaves crackling as he turned the page. Then he began to read from the book in a soft, gentle voice, that I knew to be Eappa's:

'Brand, ever are the faithful tormented by the spirits of evil and the hearts and minds of the people are persuaded by the devil that these spirits should be revered as true gods. Strength in faith and psalms sung fervently drive away the spirits, yet people still fear them. Go into the world of spirits, Brand, for you do it in the name and service of the Lord. Do not be afraid of their terrible appearance, their shrieks and moans, for the will of the Lord is with you. To protect the flock of the faithful you must enter what seems to be the den of wolves. Learn their ways and see that they too go with the blessing of the Almighty.'

I awoke suddenly with a start. It was still dark and I felt that I had been asleep only a few moments. I tried to collect my thoughts for I knew now what I must do: it was the Will of the Almighty that I go with Wulf and learn the ways of his spirits. And as soon as the resolve passed into my mind, I felt an uncanny sense of security and well-being. The terrors of the night were extinguished like snuffed candles. I thought at first that I was enjoying the relief of having made the decision, but gradually it dawned upon me that I was feeling the excitement of anticipation. It was not just a matter of duty or loyalty to Eappa, nor even the undoubted joy of serving the Lord. Rather, the secrets of the spirits seemed to beckon to me and the surrounding forest tingled with excitement and challenge. Above, the pagan sky floated blue as turquoise, silver stars twinkling like jewelled icons and the moon pouring down light like a heaven full of altar candles. The thunder god had withdrawn and the Lord was blessing my Mission.

4

UNLEASHING LIFE-FORCE

I AWOKE to the soft, pearly light of dawn. Wulf was sitting on the fallen oak, watching me.

'I have been waiting for you to return,' he said genially.

'Return?' I mumbled, my tongue thick with sleep.

'From your dreams.'

I had slept heavily and I sat up slowly, easing my stiff neck. Wulf gestured towards his hat which was lying upturned on the ground, brimming with red berries. From my bag I took the remainder of the barley bread, now rock hard inside its linen wrap, and broke off a piece for him. We sucked at it between mouthfuls of the tart berries.

'I am coming with you,' I said, a glimmer of pride in my voice. It had not been an easy decision to make.

Wulf nodded, sucking berry juice from his fingers.

'I know. We shall begin today by hunting, before the sun rides high.'

Slightly irritated by his pretence of already knowing my decision, I sulked in silence for a while. But I was intrigued by the prospect of hunting. I had not hunted since I was a boy, not even for rabbits, for the monastery gardens provided barter for all our food needs.

'What will we hunt, Wulf?' I asked, feigning indifference.

'Plants.'

I looked at him blankly.

'I always hunt the early summer plants,' he said, as if his statement explained the strange proposal.

My enthusiasm drained away. Many back-breaking hours spent shuffling up and down the monastic herb gardens, weeding between neat rows of rosemary and fennel, had left me a less than avid collector of plants.

I pulled a long stalk of grass and chewed the moist end to cleanse my mouth of the bitter taste of the berries.

'What plants do you collect, Wulf?' I asked listlessly, thinking that the information might be useful to the Mission.

Wulf leaned forward and ran a freckled hand thoughtfully through his beard.

'Well, there are many. Sometimes I collect the rootbeds of wild iris, hunting especially for those in full purple flower, with veins of deep colour running through the petals. Also, I dig the jagged-leaf wild radish and the carline thistle – taking the whole plant, roots, petal-shaped bracts, white flowers and stems. Also white cowbane and dropwort are useful, especially when collected from mossy stream banks. I have taken yellow celandine for particular purposes, but only plants with four-petalled flowers on long stalks. The grey stems give an orange-coloured honey which is very powerful medicine. The blue, pink and purple hooded houndstooth have especially potent leaves, which when crushed smell of mice. But the root, when prepared for sorcery, is very powerful indeed.'

Wulf paused, cocking an eyebrow at me. I was trying to commit to memory as many plants as possible.

'Then there is hassock,' he continued, smiling, 'and yewberry, lupine, elecampane – preferably cut when it is at man-height – dwarf-elder, the heads of marshmallow, fen-mint, dill, lily, cockspur grass, horehound, bitter wormwood, starry stitchwort, woodruff, honey-scented crosswort . . .'

Wulf started to laugh at me and I realised that my face was twisted into a grimace of concentration. He had been talking so quickly that I was having difficulty in following his dialect, let alone recognising and memorising the plants.

'The names of these plants mean nothing,' Wulf chuckled. 'They each have to be specially prepared, with plants known only to sorcerers. Even to begin to learn about the plants of power, you must collect and prepare them with me, not memorise their names!'

I laughed with relief. I could remember only about five or six of the plants he had listed, and these were plants already known to the Mission. Indeed, for the monastic library I had transcribed sections from volumes of the classical Greek herbals. But I was interested in Wulf's reference to plants of power.

'Plants of power are important allies for a sorcerer,' he said, as if reading my thoughts. 'With their aid I can influence the life-force of a person.'

'Life-force?' The term meant nothing to me.

'Life-force permeates everything. It is the source of all vitality. In a person it is generated in the head, flows like a stream of light into the marrow of the spine and from there into the limbs and crevices of the body. Power-plants help to control the channels through which the energy flows.'

I was intrigued by the idea, but could not conceive of its material essence. I tried to picture it as a liquid substance.

'Is life-force like blood?' I asked.

Wulf shook his head. 'Life-force is visible only to a sorcerer. However, you do not need a sorcerer to be aware of your own life-force, for there are occasions when even an ordinary person generates vast quantities of it. For example, life-force increases when you are ill. Serious illness is a sign that spirits are attacking your soul. But usually spirits cannot capture a soul which is protected by life-force and at the first signs of danger life-force blazes into your head like a furnace. The inner heat is so great that your head will feel hot, even to the touch of others. If the spirits continue their attack, life-force flows down the spine like molten metal in a smith's crucible and the entire body becomes hot. Even if the spirits successfully capture the victim's soul, life-force continues to rage in an attempt to keep the body intact until the soul can be returned. But if a sorcerer does not intervene to recapture the soul, the sick person will burn himself out like a forest fire, and die.'

Wulf's graphic account reminded me of a serious illness I had survived as a small boy. I had been so hot I could hardly breathe, and my head had felt as if it were on fire. Terrifying voices and demons had visited me. Prayers had been said for me, to no avail, but one night my father had brought an old man from the village who examined me by looking into my ears. He had poured an evil-smelling substance on to my head and body and then sung strange words to me. The following day I cooled down and gradually recovered completely. I remember my father telling everyone in the family never to breathe a word about the old man's visit to the house, because we lived on monastic property and the priests would be angry.

It surprised me that I had completely forgotten the incident until now, but I said nothing about it to Wulf. I sat and watched him cleaning berry juice from his hat with dew-wet bunches of grass.

'Did you see the slaves at Aethelwealh's fortress?' Wulf enquired suddenly.

I nodded, puzzled by the question.

'Did you see the metal bands around their necks? These bands signify that the slave's life-force does not flow freely into his body, for his vitality is controlled by his owner. And the beard and hair of slaves is cropped, for hair is one of the outward signs of life-force in a person.'

Wulf put on his black hat, pushed it to the back of his head and looked at me with half-closed eyes. In the soft light one of his eyes appeared strangely misty and his gaze made me feel distinctly uncomfortable.

'You are young and healthy, Brand. You are generating abundant life-force, but it does not flow freely. You are blocking it.'

I laughed with embarrassment and self-consciously passed a hand over my close-cropped hair.

'No, Wulf. Short hair is the custom for the Brethren of my faith. My life is dedicated to Almighty God, but I am a slave to no man of this world.'

Wulf shook his head slowly, still looking at me probingly. 'I shall arrange for you to meet Water Goddess. She will unleash your life-force.'

'What do you mean, Wulf? What is the Water Goddess?' I was as alarmed by his sly demeanour as I was by his reference to the goddess.

'Water Goddess is beautiful,' he said, a crafty gleam in his eyes. 'She is soft and warm; she will wrap you in her silvery embrace and your spirit will rise.'

He made what I took to be an obscene gesture and I turned away from him in disgust, feeling my face flush with anger. I was acutely embarrassed by such talk. Sometimes I had whispered about such matters with the novices in the dormitory, but to discuss it openly with a stranger was shameful. I made much of undoing and restrapping my shoes, hoping that Wulf would drop the subject.

I could sense that he was watching me but I sat in frosty silence, staring at my shoes. Suddenly he squatted next to me and thrust his face into mine.

'In this Kingdom, a lover is called a neck-bedfellow, because after being with a woman you can virtually feel the bonds of enslavement around your neck.' He wagged a forefinger sternly. 'A woman will draw the life-energy from you and sap your strength. You are absolutely right to be so careful.'

I looked at him in surprise. His face, inches from mine, was creased with concern and sincerity. I had erroneously believed that he was going to mock my lack of sexual experience, but now he sounded exactly like Eappa, warning of the temptations of the flesh. It was all the more remarkable in that I had been told that pagan practitioners of sorcery used their status to indulge in disgraceful sexual licence.

'Does this mean that, like the Brethren of my faith, you do not lie with women? That you were joking about the Water Goddess?'

Suddenly Wulf's demeanour changed and he looked down at the ground, shuffling about nervously. With horror I realised that I had embarrassed him and had risen half-way to my feet to apologise when I saw a sly smile spread across his face. I was caught between sitting and standing when he exploded into laughter.

I sat down and glared at him, feeling utterly ridiculous. He had led me to commit myself on a matter of considerable personal sensitivity and I thought him crass and inconsiderate in the extreme.

Still chuckling, Wulf crouched by my side and put an arm around my shoulders.

'Do not worry!' he chuckled. 'If you are going to encounter Water Goddess, I shall give you advance warning so that you may seek forgiveness from your god.'

I turned towards him to retort angrily: he was struggling to control his mirth but as I looked into his eyes, I felt a wave of warmth from him, even affection. I laughed nervously.

'We are taught to stay away from the pleasures of the flesh,' I said ruefully.

He nodded gently, still with an arm around me. 'Life-force pulses from Mother Earth when she is kissed by the Spring Sun. So it is between man and woman. Sexual love is essential for a free flow of life-force. Just as frost and fire create the worlds, so man and woman create life.'

Wulf clapped me on the back and stood up. 'But we shall worry about Water Goddess another time. Enough about your neck – it is time to hunt.'

We gathered together our things and Wulf led the way into the forest. Our path snaked northwards through miles of dense forest, Wulf tracking animal paths barely visible in the thick undergrowth and moving with the superb agility of a deer. Above the tree cover the sky was a haze of high cloud, and in air warm and moist as steam my clothes clung to me in sticky streaks. I was soon hampered not only by my lack of forest-walking experience but also by the nagging pain in my ankle; resting had not healed it and each step brought with it the awful memory of the horse-head dream.

Eventually we followed a stream bank into a shallow ravine, until the path narrowed to a mere strip of chalky footholds barely covered by tufts of dry grass. The western face of the ravine towered above us to our left, and Wulf stopped to point out a switchback route up the steep face of the hill. He climbed swiftly and I scrambled after him, clawing for footholds which frequently broke away under my weight. At last I pulled myself on to the grassy plateau at the top and stretched out on the ground beside Wulf, gulping air into my burning lungs. When I sat up, I realised how high we had climbed. On the northern horizon, rising above the treeline, I could see the tips of distant hills reaching towards a huge sky and as I watched, the high clouds pulled apart to admit glimmers of weak, pale, yellow sunlight.

After a short rest, Wulf led the way across the thickly turfed plateau. He walked slowly, apparently scanning the grass, until he stopped abruptly. In front of us a scattering of yellow flowers barely peeped above the grass, blowing in the wind. I had never before seen such plants.

'What are they called?' I asked tentatively, afraid to interrupt the intense concentration with which Wulf was surveying the flowers.

He bent down on one knee and plucked a sprig from the plant nearest to him.

'Do not label them; just get to know them,' he said. 'Here, chew this piece.'

He handed me a leaf. I put it on my tongue and sucked at it cautiously.

'Chew it!' Wulf instructed, watching me closely.

I bit into it and immediately my mouth stung with an unpleasantly bitter taste. I spat it out into my palm.

'What do you use it for?' I asked, wiping my tongue with my fingers to relieve the burning sensation.

Ignoring the question, Wulf stepped carefully into the cluster of plants; squatting next to one, he cradled a leaf in his palm and laid the first and middle fingers together above the leaf.

'See? It is too small,' he said. 'Take only those that are broader than your two fingers. We need the most vigorous plants.'

He pulled his knife from his leather sheath and, thinking we were about to cut some plants, I moved to a large plant three or four paces away and slipped my hand under a leaf near the base. It was almost as broad as three fingers. I grasped the top of the plant and unsheathed my knife.

'No!' Wulf's sharp cry froze me and he leaped over and grasped my wrist. 'First we must mark them.'

While I watched carefully he rested the long blade of his knife in his left palm, curled his fingers around it and with a sudden twist flicked the blade against his fingers. When he opened his hand, blood was seeping from the fleshy underside of his fingers and dribbling into his palm. The warning notes of nearby sparrows pierced my ears with unnerving clarity and a wave of apprehension stirred in my stomach.

Sheathing the knife, Wulf crouched over one of the yellow flowers, examining it closely, his face a mask of concentration. I watched him in trepidation, helpless to intervene. He rubbed his fingers against one of the leaves, smearing blood all along the stem and across the leaf. A stench of evil pervaded the plateau and, sickened, I turned away trying to control the urge to retch. Christian teachings and law expressly forbade blood rituals and in silent anger I berated myself for not having realised that I might be an unwitting witness to such abominations.

Wulf repeated the disgusting ritual with two more plants, while I stared determinedly into the distance, trying to separate myself from his activities. Then he rose to his feet and stepped away from the plants to stand at my side. I clamped my jaw shut, determined to voice no protest but simply to report all I could to the Mission.

Wulf calmly surveyed the expanse of yellow flowers. 'We identify the best specimens and offer them our blood,' he said, almost in a whisper. 'When we have finished, we shall take only those plants marked by our blood.'

He pulled out his knife and again laid the blade across his left palm, then nodded towards my own knife. With horror and dismay, I realised that he intended that I should cut my fingers also. The evil prospect filled me with dread.

'Why do we need to mark them, Wulf?' I stammered, searching desperately for an excuse which would not offend him 'If we test them for size, then cut them immediately, we cannot forget which plants we want to collect.'

Wulf stared at me steadily, unblinking.

'Identifying them is not the purpose,' he said in a voice as soft as the wind. 'The blood is your sacrifice to the plant.'

I looked around in panic, seeing no alternative to a confrontation. 'But the blood . . . I am not able to spill my blood on the plants. It is forbidden to those of my faith.'

Wulf arched his eyebrows. 'Do you not offer blood sacrifice to your god, Brand?'

He gazed directly at me, his eyes confident, unwavering, knowing. Immediately I thought of the Eucharist, in which we take bread together with wine and, after consecration, they become through a spiritual mystery truly Christ's body and his blood. But I could not believe that Wulf would know of our ritual – and even if he did, he could not understand it.

'No. We don't,' I said firmly.

'Do you not drink the blood of your god?' Wulf persisted, his eyes twinkling now with amusement. 'I am not asking you to drink the blood of your god, merely to dedicate a small drop of your own in honour of the plants.'

I thought now that surely he knew of the Eucharist, for he was baiting me with wicked enjoyment.

'But Wulf, this is different. We are not here worshipping my God or your gods; we are merely picking flowers.'

'We are not picking flowers like some courting lover,' Wulf snapped, his eyes flashing with sudden anger. 'We are hunting for power. If we were merely picking leaves, flowers or berries the plant would not suffer, for it could replace them. But we are about to take the roots of these plants, for therein lies the source of their life-force. When we dig a plant from the ground, we have separated it from its source of breath, and it can no longer spin a spirit-skin. The plant will die because we have laid a claim on its life-force, and we have to offer something of ourselves in return. Our blood is a gift to the plant, a token of our thanks.'

'But Wulf, such concern is reasonable for the death of a person, for people are divinely blessed. But how can you feel so strongly about plants?'

'Plants carry life-force as potent as any person. To take the life of a plant, whether for food or sorcery, is to act with the gods.'

I snorted condescendingly. Everything Wulf said underlined the error of his ways; at the monastery we blessed the fields and prayed for the favour of the Almighty in growing our crops. But we did not, of course, harvest plant foods as if taking life, for plants and animals were provided by God for use by man.

Wulf gestured impatiently towards my knife – and this time I said nothing. I knew that I had either to refuse and lose Wulf's services as my guide, or to suspend my beliefs in the higher service of the Lord. It had to be the latter course. I was here to listen, learn and report to the Mission, not to argue the teachings of the Lord; that blessed task would be carried out by others in good time. I had to believe that no matter what I did in this God-forsaken land, I was acting to his greater glory. Wulf's blood ritual would be, for me, a sacrifice to the Almighty.

I laid the knife across my palm, closed my eyes and prayed

silently for His forgiveness. Gingerly, I pressed the cold blade into my fingers and nicked the two middle fingers near the base. Blood oozed out slowly and trickled between my fingers.

To my surprise, Wulf suddenly put an arm around my shoulders and hugged me gently. 'Now let us collect some power,' he said, leading me by the arm into the cluster of plants. We crouched down next to a large plant.

'Mark them like this,' Wulf instructed. 'Grip the plant tightly, placing your thumb and forefinger around a leaf.' He held a leaf with a pincer movement of his fingers and deftly stroked a line of blood down the centre vein.

I took hold of a leaf and bent it over carefully. The plant exuded a heavy, musty odour as I pulled the leaf taut and wiped it with my palm. It made only the faintest streak of red because the blood on my hand had dried, but even so I felt nauseated and thought I was going to be sick.

Wulf materialised at my side.

'All the plants are trying to help you,' he said cheerfully, indicating with a sweep of his arm the expanse of flowers on the plateau. 'Listen! They are talking loudly to you.'

I looked around at the yellow petal clusters, bending and ducking in the breeze.

'See? They are all waving at you,' Wulf said, chuckling.

The very idea of flowers waving to me was amusing enough to break the tension and I sucked in several deep breaths.

'Now cut harder and collect the blood in your palm,' Wulf instructed, still crouched at my side.

Again I pushed in the blade, feeling the cutting edge slicing into my fingers. This time blood gushed at an alarming rate and ran warm into my cupped hand.

Squatting still, I hurriedly wiped my hand against the plant, blood streaking an incongruously bright red against the dull green of the leaf. But the leaves were still moist from night dew and the blood gradually diluted and faded to a pale pink smudge.

I forced myself to mark a second plant and this time I felt less nauseated, though my cut fingers now stung sharply. I had just finished marking my fourth plant when Wulf's voice broke the silence and he called me over to watch him.

'Brand, we have marked enough. Let us now take the marked

plants. We must take out the entire plant; use your knife to dig a circle in the ground, about a foot from the plant, but take care not to cut the roots.'

Working swiftly, he dug a trench round a plant he had marked, then inserted his fingers into the circular depression and forced them deeper, eventually working his fingers under the root and lifting the whole plant from the ground.

I set to work on the first plant I had marked. The task was absorbing and difficult, for the rain-soaked soil was heavy. Eventually I raised the plant and, carefully concealing from him my sense of achievement, submitted it to Wulf for inspection.

'See where you have injured it,' he said, pointing to a subsidiary root that had snapped off.

I looked at it closely. It was only a tiny break. 'But Wulf, the plant is almost intact. I pulled it from the ground very carefully.'

Wulf shook his head. 'You chopped through that root with your knife. Life-force is drawn off by iron. A plant which has been cut with iron is no longer a plant of power and is useless to a sorcerer.'

He insisted that I replace the plant in the exact spot from which I had taken it.

We worked for a while longer and Wulf accepted two of the four plants I raised, placing them carefully in a large sack and closing the top. I noticed that he stowed away into a separate sack the plants he had dug up.

Wulf placed the sacks carefully in the shade, in a hollow at the base of a lone beech. The sun had risen high in the sky and we stretched out to rest under the tree. I decided to try again for more information.

'Wulf, what will you use the plants for?'

'Venoms,' he replied casually.

I sat up and glanced around nervously. I was always on the alert for adders, for their bite was deadly.

'What kind of venoms?' I asked, trying – and failing – to adopt a matter-of-fact tone.

Wulf could not fail to notice that I was looking with consternation into the grass.

'Snakes more powerful than you have ever encountered,' he chuckled. 'In these forests, some snakes mediate between death and life. They carry the life-force leaked from the dead until it is taken up by another living form. We can expect snakes to follow us for a while, seeking the life-force from the plants in those sacks. But we have marked them with our blood and therefore have first claim on the life-force. For a time, anyway, the snakes cannot harm the plants.'

He had not really answered my question. I wanted to hear how the snakes could affect me.

'Wulf, according to your beliefs, do the snakes ever approach dying people?'

He nodded lazily. 'And they approach living people; that is why the bite of some snakes is so deadly. They thirst for the life-force of other creatures and if none is presented to them they sometimes seek it out for themselves. If a snake kills you, your soul is released from your life-force and flies around screaming through the world of the dead, burning like a flame in the night.'

I swallowed hard. I found his images very disturbing.

'The plants are meant to protect from such forces?' I asked.

'Yes, eventually. In the meantime, we should keep you clear of the dealers in death.'

I glanced at him in time to see him smile. He seemed to treat the death of people more lightly than the death of plants. With a finger to his lips he cut off my next question before I had mouthed it.

'Let us start,' he said. 'I want to reach Cydda's farm by nightfall, and we may have more work to do before then.'

He gave me the sack containing my own two plants.

'Do not allow the sack to drag on the ground or bump into the trees,' he warned. 'The plants are very delicate and any injury to the roots will render them useless.'

Wulf led the way north, across the plateau and into thin copses of mixed beech and oak woodland. Gradually the land sloped down into a valley and we rejoined the stream that had cut through the ravine. Then we tracked north-west, away from the stream.

As we walked, I tried to order my thoughts. Guilt about what I had done gnawed at my stomach. I tried to concentrate on the positive aspects, itemising in my mind the information I could report to the Mission. First, I attempted to recall some of the plants Wulf had listed as being of use to him. Then I rehearsed, over and over, the plant collecting ritual as I would report it to Brother Eappa. But, hard as I tried, the Mission seemed distant not only in miles and days but also in spirit. Wulf trudged into thick forest and increasingly, as the terrain became more entangled with undergrowth, my thoughts were distracted by stabs of pain from the ankle. I tried to favour it and eventually limped quite badly, concealing the limp from Wulf whenever he turned round to wait for me. I concentrated so hard on controlling the pain that I almost forgot where I was, cocooned in my own world.

'Stop!'

Wulf's cry startled me and I froze immediately, looking around in alarm. We were about a third of the way across a small meadow, set in the forest like an island in a sea of trees. I scanned the ground rapidly, searching for the zigzag back of an adder.

'Don't move!' Wulf ordered. He was crouching about five paces away, staring at my feet. He crawled carefully around me like a wildcat ready to pounce, coming no closer than five paces.

'What's the matter, Wulf?' I said, completely bewildered. My voice sounded small and frightened and seemed to come from a long way away.

'Look at the grass in front of you,' he hissed and obediently I stared at the ground.

Wulf's intensity was making me feel panicky, but I could see nothing in the grass. He rose slowly to his feet, standing on the balls of his feet and balanced for rapid movement. Pointing in front of me, he moved his arm to indicate a circular area on the ground.

Immediately I became aware of a circular patch of grass, about three or four paces in diameter, which was longer and darker than the surrounding meadowland. Inside the circle was a small patch of bare earth and at the centre, a cluster of small, strange mushroom-shaped plants, their bright red caps covered in white patches.

'We are in a power field,' Wulf warned, holding up one hand to keep me motionless. 'If you had walked into those plants the concentration of power would have struck you down like a bolt of lightning.'

I stood stock-still, staring at the plants. I had seen them before and knew that some peasants believed them to have special powers. Eappa taught that such notions were absurd, but I had no desire whatever to challenge this now. The red mushrooms loomed in my vision like deadly flames. Slowly and carefully, I backed out of the circle.

'The spirits are aware of your presence,' Wulf muttered ominously, darting glances into the surrounding shrubbery. 'They are the key to the secrets of Middle-Earth, for they have access to the gods and the Underworld. In these sacks, we have the means to make enough life-force to protect you from the excesses of the spirits, but you are not yet ready for it. In the meantime, we must be very careful, for the spirits are testing you. The power circle was a trap. Walk close behind me and do not speak until I tell you that we are clear of the danger.'

Wulf set off at a slower pace and I followed so closely we were almost touching. I put my hand to my chest to feel the comforting shape of my crucifix. Beside it, I could feel my heart pounding, but I knew that there could now be no turning back.

5

READING THE OMENS OF WYRD

WULF WADED knee-deep into the water, paddled up river and disappeared around a bend. I settled back to wait for him. It was a tranquil scene. Trees leaned drunkenly from opposite banks to meet above the river and weak sunlight, slanting through the foliage, shimmered and danced among the shadows on the water. White and pale yellow parsley covered the bank sides and smothered the roots of the trees. Finches, tree pipits and blackbirds flitted and sang amongst flowering shrubs. The setting was so calm that I found it difficult to believe that this same forest had held such terrors for me during the night.

After collecting the plants, we had trudged on without further incident until the sun passed its high point in the sky when, drenched with sweat, we had stopped to rest by a river bank. My injured ankle had been agony and frequently I had failed to keep up the pace even though I was desperate to stay close behind Wulf. Several times he had waited for me to catch up with him.

'Do you always hop on one leg?' he said finally, pointing to my ankle.

'I twisted it, getting over one of those storm-fall trees,' I said untruthfully. While accepting that Wulf somehow knew about the demons I had encountered, I still had not been able to accept the fact that my ankle had been damaged during the terrifying horse-head dream.

Wulf took my arm and helped me to hobble from the path, through some bushes and on to the river bank.

'Show me the injury,' he said, lowering me into a clump of

purple heather. I sank down gratefully, unstrapped my shoe and peeled back the leggings. The ankle was swollen and throbbed steadily; I fingered it gingerly, wincing with pain.

Wulf squatted next to me and looked closely at the damaged ankle, cradling it gently in his palm. He lowered my foot carefully to the ground and grunted, nodding his head knowingly.

'Stay there and do not move,' he instructed. 'I shall return shortly.'

At that point Wulf had paddled up the river. Now, waiting for him to return, I leaned back on my elbows and yawned indulgently. As I tipped my head back, I glimpsed the tiny silhouette of a hunting hawk gliding across the clear, early afternoon sky. While I watched it, the bird dropped out of the blue and hurtled towards me like an arrow. I snapped fully alert, startled, but then the bird seemed to veer away and shot out of sight behind the trees. The sky was empty, as if the hawk had never existed.

I sat up with my heart pounding, feeling foolish. The incident with the power circle had obviously left me nervous and insecure. I tried to control myself and waited impatiently for Wulf to return.

Eventually he appeared around the bend in the river and I breathed easily again. When he splashed on to the bank, I could see that he was carrying fistfuls of large, dark green leaves which had spiked edges and a rough, hairy surface.

'What are the leaves Wulf?'

He knelt down, cautiously lifted my foot and rested it on his knee. The leaves had apparently been soaked in the river and he slapped them one by one on to my ankle, like wet fish.

'Your ankle was injured in a spirit-dream and needs special attention,' he said, without looking up from his work. 'These leaves are from a plant known only to sorcerers.'

I glared at him with a mixture of anger and awe. There seemed no limit to his knowledge of my affairs.

'There! Now you can run like a deer!' he said emphatically, applying the last of the leaves and binding them to my ankle with a strip of cloth taken from his bag. Then he stood up and held out a hand to help me to my feet.

'Let us cool ourselves in the river,' he said, striding down to the water's edge.

I limped to the bank and waded eagerly into the fast, cold current. At first the chill took my breath away, then it was exhilarating. I heard Wulf splashing into the river behind me and turned, laughing, in time to see him emerging from complete submersion like some river monster, water streaming from the end of his nose and glistening on his eyelashes.

Suddenly he stared past me up river, his smile stiffening into a frown. I followed his gaze towards a copse of trees on the south bank, but saw nothing unusual. I blinked my eyes clear of river water however, and immediately noticed two huge black ravens in the lower branches of a weeping willow, perched perfectly motionless like creatures in a tapestry. Their very stillness gripped me with a strange fascination. I could not shift my eyes from them; gradually the forest sounds receded into the distance as if I were slipping into a dream.

The ravens flapped enormous silent wings, lifted into the air and flew down river straight towards me, but they continued to speed low over the water and, at the very last moment, I had to duck my head beneath the surface. The ravens passed inches above me, their wings beating like the great, groaning oars of raiding ships. Gasping and spitting river water, I turned to watch them fly away from us like arrows until both ravens simultaneously stilled their wings, drifted upward on the wind, dipped again and then glided towards the north bank of the river. Abruptly they disappeared and I stared in bewilderment at the spot where they had vanished.

'Death's bonds will stalk someone tonight.'

I started at the sound of Wulf's voice, then my ears popped and the sounds of the forest clanged back into my head like a chapel bell.

'The ravens have spoken to us,' Wulf said severely, wading to my side. 'When birds fly like that it is a powerful omen. A warrior will die tonight.'

I had been truly startled by the strange flight of the birds, but I smiled to myself when I heard Wulf's ludicrous claim, recalling that in my Mercian homeland the peasants superstitiously associated ravens with death. Brother Eappa had taught me the error of such beliefs and that the Lord is truly the only giver and taker of life.

'There is no destiny apart from the Almighty Creator,' I said firmly.

'Are there no other forces?' Wulf asked mildly. 'What about the destiny of the stars?'

I snorted with derision, though I tried to temper my reply.

'There are some, who know no better, who say that every man is born according to the position of the stars and that his destiny befalls him as a result of their course. But man is not created for the stars; rather, the stars are created for man as a light in night time. If this is true of the stars, then how can the mere flight of birds tell us about events distant in time and place?'

Eappa would have been pleased; I must have quoted his teachings practically word for word. I turned to wade ashore, but Wulf suddenly gripped my by the arm and I looked at him in alarm; he was looking at me piercingly, his eyes clear azure blue through lashes sparkling with river water. He spoke with conviction:

'It is a mistake to assume that events far apart in time are thereby separate. All things are connected as in the finest web of a spider. The slightest movement on any thread can be discerned from all points in the web. The flight of those ravens trembled the threads that connect indivisibly with the affairs of men.'

My scepticism must have been plainly visible in my expression. 'Wulf, are you saying that the ravens we have just seen will kill a warrior tonight?'

With the hint of a smile, Wulf released his grip on my arm and splashed on to the river bank. I stood in the water, watching him.

'Imagine you were to witness a raven swooping from the sky to peck out the eye of a warrior,' he said, stretching out on the grass. 'You would say that the flight of the bird was connected directly with the wound. But if you had observed the flight of the same raven half a day before the attack, you would see no connection with the warrior's injury. Nevertheless the pattern of a raven's flight at noon is bound to the pattern of its flight at dusk, just as surely as the progression of day and night. One can read the pattern and thus see what the future has in store.'

He sat up and stared at me intently.

'You are labelling pieces of the world with words, then confusing your word-hoard for the totality of life. You see life as if you were viewing a room by the light of a single moving candle; then you make the error of assuming that the small areas you are seeing one at a time are separate and cannot be seen as one. Since the small areas of your life are thus seen as separate, you have to invent ways of connecting them. This is the fallacy of the ordinary person's view of life, for everything is already connected. Middle-Earth is one room, lit by a thousand candles.'

I sat in silence, impressed by the beauty of Wulf's flawed view of life. But behind his words, I found his argument absurd. I glanced up river into the sun, slanting through silvery-grey clouds. Suddenly my eye caught the brilliant red and blue flash of a kingfisher and I watched it darting above the water until it disappeared around the river bend. I could see no pattern or significance in its flight.

I waded from the river and sat down wetly next to Wulf.

'Do you really believe that you can read future events from a tiny snatch of bird flight? Do all your people believe in such omens?'

Wulf rolled on to his back and cupped his hands behind his head, squinting up at the sky.

'Omens frighten the ordinary person because they believe them to be predictions of events that are bound to happen: warnings from the realms of destiny. But this is to mistake the true nature of omens. A sorcerer can read omens as pattern-pointers, from which the weaving of wyrd can be admired and from which connections between different parts of patterns can be assumed.'

I was puzzled by his use of the term 'wyrd'. When used by monks orating poetry, it seemed to denote the destiny or fate of a person. I explained this view to Wulf and he hooted with laughter, sending the sparrows flapping from the shrubbery in alarm.

'To understand our ways, you must learn the true meaning of wyrd, not the version your masters have concocted to fit their beliefs. Remember that I told you our world began with fire and frost? By themselves, neither fire nor frost accomplish anything. But together they create the world. Yet they must maintain a balance, for too much fire would melt the frost and excessive frost would extinguish the fire. But just as the worlds of gods, Middle-Earth and the Dead are constantly replenished by the marrying of fire and frost, so also they depend upon the balance and eternal cycle of night and day, winter and summer, woman and man, weak and strong, moon and sun, death and life. These forces, and countless others, form the end points of a gigantic web of fibres which covers all worlds. The web is the creation of the forces and its threads, shimmering with power, pass through everything.'

I was astounded by the image of the web, which seemed to me both stupendous and terrifying. I trembled with excitement, for I knew that Eappa would drink in such information like a hunter pinpointing the movements of his prey.

'What is at the centre of the web, Wulf? Are your gods at the centre?'

Wulf smiled, a little condescendingly I thought.

'You may start at any point on the web and find that you are at the centre,' he said cryptically.

Disappointed, I tried another line of questioning. 'Is wyrd your most important god?'

'No. Wyrd existed before the gods and will exist after them. Yet wyrd lasts only for an instant, because it is the constant creation of the forces. Wyrd is itself constant change, like the seasons, yet because it is created at every instant it is unchanging, like the still centre of a whirlpool. All we can see are the ripples dancing on top of the water.'

I stared at him in complete confusion. His concept of wyrd, obviously of vital importance to him, repeatedly slipped through my fingers like an eel. I went back to the beginning of our conversation.

'But Wulf, you say that the flight of birds shows you the pattern of wyrd, of these fibres; if you can predict events from wyrd, it must then operate according to certain laws?'

Wulf looked at me with kind, friendly eyes. He seemed to be enjoying my attempts to understand his mysterious ideas.

'No, Brand, there are no laws. The pattern of wyrd is like the grain in wood, or the flow of a stream; it is never repeated in exactly the same way. But the threads of wyrd pass through all things and we can open ourselves to its pattern by observing the ripples as it passes by. When you see ripples in a pool, you know that something has dropped into the water. And when I see certain ripples in the flight of birds, I know that a warrior is going to die.'

'So wyrd makes things happen?'

'Nothing may happen without wyrd, for it is present in everything, but wyrd does not *make* things happen. Wyrd is created at every instant, and so wyrd *is* the happening.'

Suddenly I tired of his cryptic responses. 'I suppose the threads of wyrd are too fine for anyone to *see*?' I said sarcastically.

Wulf chuckled goodnaturedly. 'Sometimes they are thick as hemp rope. But the threads of wyrd are a dimension of ourselves that we cannot grasp with words. We spin webs of words, yet wyrd slips through like the wind. The secrets of wyrd do not lie in our word-hoards, but are locked in the soul. We can only discern the shadows of reality with our words, whereas our souls are capable of encountering the realities of wyrd directly. This is why wyrd is accessible to the sorcerer: the sorcerer sees with his soul, not with eyes blinkered by the shape of words.'

I knew Wulf's views to be erroneous, yet I was fascinated by them. He spoke about his beliefs as confidently and fluently as Eappa explaining the teachings of our Saviour. I rested my chin on my hands and tried to analyse Wulf's ideas as Eappa would have wished. 'Be sure you understand clearly everything you see and hear,' he had cautioned. 'You can remember only what you comprehend.' I tried to identify the main tenets of Wulf's beliefs and subject them to scrutiny, one by one.

Wulf leaned closer to me and spoke into my ear as if sharing a secret:

'You are strangling you life-force with words. Do not live your life searching around for answers in your word-hoard. You will find only words to rationalise your experience. Allow yourself to open up to wyrd and it will cleanse, renew, change and develop your casket of reason. Your word-hoard should serve your experience, not the reverse.'

I turned on him in irritation. 'I was chosen for this Mission because I do not swallow everything I hear like a simpleton. I am at home in the world of words.'

He smiled gently. 'Words can be potent magic indeed, but they can also enslave us. We grasp from wyrd tiny puffs of wind and store them in our lungs as words. But we have not thereby captured a piece of reality, to be pored over and examined as if it were a glimpse of wyrd. We may as well mistake our fistfuls of air for wind itself, or a pitcher of water for the stream from which it was dipped. That is the way we are enslaved by our own power to name things.'

'My thoughts are my personal affair,' I said sulkily. I was here to listen to his beliefs, but not to submit to criticism of my private contemplation.

'Thoughts are like raindrops,' he persisted, introducing yet another of his interminable images. 'They fall, make a splash and then dry up. But the world of wyrd is like the mighty oceans from which raindrops arise and to which they return in rivers and streams.'

Suddenly Wulf sat up, as though he had just thought of something important. 'What did the runes say? The ones carved under the horse's head?'

I went cold. I no longer believed that I could conceal from Wulf any of that night's horrors, but the memory of my nightmare was still painful.

'I would rather not talk about it, Wulf. I do not see what benefit it would bring to either of us.'

'But it *is* important,' Wulf insisted. He spoke quietly, but his eyes bored into me relentlessly.

'Runes are another path to the mysteries of wyrd, more powerful even than omens. The runes carved on the horse-stake may have been a message for you from the spirits. Did you see any marks or symbols carved into the post?'

I tried to force the image into my mind, but concentrating only gave me a splitting headache.

'I cannot remember them, Wulf. There were some carvings on the post, but I do not recall what they looked like.'

'You must try to remember. The runes on that stake may help us to determine the spirits' attitude towards us and to gauge their intentions.'

I was suddenly angry. Learning from Wulf was not only

proving very taxing but his apparent ability to see into my dreams was totally demoralising.

'Surely you saw the runes,' I snapped. 'You seem to have seen everything else.'

'Tell me about the runes,' he repeated quietly, ignoring my childish outburst. 'Your safety in this forest may depend upon our reading those runes.'

'I cannot tell you about the runes,' I shouted. 'I do not understand them. We are not allowed to work with them.'

In Mercia runes were now officially outlawed, though peasants still unlawfully carved them on sticks and threw them as lotteries, foretelling the future. Brother Eappa knew how to read and write runic inscriptions, but they were forbidden to initiates in the scriptorium for they were sacriligious.

'All I know is that each runic character represents a sound, and beginning with each sound is a word of significance.'

Wulf nodded once in agreement, then reached over and placed his hand on my shoulder. 'All right, forget about the runes on the horse head stake,' he said in a reassuring tone. 'We shall deal with those later. But let me tell you about runes, so that you will not make another mistake when presented with a message from the spirit-world.'

He sat, cross-legged, facing me.

'Rune images are like the shifting cloud-shapes of wyrd,' he explained. 'The dimensions and formation of each rune can be learned by anyone, but the way in which a set of runes is interpreted in a particular context requires the knowledge of a sorcerer. They are not to be read like a simple set of sounds, for the runes have been evolved by the spirits by correlating all the dominant cycles and forces which course through Middle-Earth.'

He waved his arm to indicate the surrounding landscape and sky. 'Wyrd is too vast, too complex, for us to comprehend, for we are ourselves part of wyrd and cannot stand back to observe it as if it were a separate force. Just as a fisherman cannot see the full extent of the seas, so even a sorcerer cannot view the totality of wyrd. So we carve runes into wood or bone and cast them like nets on to the sea of wyrd. The messages the runes bring back are like a good catch: enough for us to feed on until the tides of life carry us back again.'

I did not like his simile, for Blessed Jesus was also a fisherman. Somehow it seemed wrong to think about pagan untruths in images reserved for the teachings of Jesus Christ our Saviour.

'Do you then think you can change the world by manipulating these symbols?' My tone was sneering; I was still upset by his implication that I had failed badly in being unable to read the runes on the stake. But I listened carefully for his answer; I wanted to learn about runes.

Wulf shook his head. 'The forces of wyrd are like the winds and tides for a fisherman. If they are known, the sailor can trim his sails to adapt to them. He can be in harmony with the forces and use their power. But he cannot thereby change them.'

Wulf stood up and with his foot scraped away grass and dandelions until he had cleared a small patch of bare earth. He picked out and threw away pebbles, sticks and other small obstructions, then smoothed the soil with the flat of his hand. Snapping off a twig from a nearby hazel shrub, he squatted next to the patch of soil and, working very rapidly, drew a series of angular shapes on the surface. When he had finished he sat back, cleaned the soil from the end of the hazel twig and then handed it to me.

'Each rune is a complete representation of wyrd. Just as one drop of water reflects a perfect image of all that is around it, so each rune reflects the totality of wyrd. The rhythm of wyrd may be observed at all levels, whether it be the movement of the stars across the sky, or the cutting of shapes into a patch of earth.'

He pointed at the set of runes spread out in front of us. 'Copy the runes I have drawn,' he instructed.

My mind raced, Eappa's warnings about the forbidden script sounding in my ears. But I forced misgivings to one side, for I had resolved that I was about the Lord's work and that anything that I did was in His service.

I leaned over, examining the sixteen figures Wulf had sketched in the soil. Excitement bubbled inside me like a spring. I felt as I had during my first days at the scriptorium, Eappa by my side, copying his calligraphy by the hour. I said a silent prayer and, with a quickening heart, began carefully copying the first runes of my life.

Rapidly the pleasure faded, however. My runes were poor and

crude copies and did not have even the fullness of shape of Wulf's. Scrawling in the dirt was not to be compared with fine quill and vellum work in the service of Almighty God.

Wulf erased my work, sweeping smooth the area under his runes. I copied them again – and again. I kept up the work, under his critical eye, until the sun began to fall from the sky. After each attempt, Wulf pointed out mistakes in great detail, sweetening the bitter taste of repeated failure with words of encouragement and praise. By the time he told me to stop for a rest, I could draw the shapes from memory and with reasonable accuracy.

Wulf stood and stretched. 'These runes are symbols of great power,' he enthused. 'I now want you to carve runes into willow, so that we can prepare a message for the spirits.'

I glanced down at my last line of runes, sitting starkly in the soil below those Wulf had written. They suddenly seemed alien, sinister and dangerous and I wanted to erase them.

'Hurry up,' Wulf called from the edge of the clearing. 'The spirits will not wait for us.'

I jumped to my feet and walked from the clearing. It was not until we were far along the trail that I remembered my injured ankle. To my surprise, it felt strong and sound. I stopped walking and stamped my foot on the ground, cautiously, experimentally. There was no pain; the ankle was healed.

I followed Wulf through the leafy glades, dappled golden by the afternoon sunlight, and eventually we emerged into an open meadow long as an arrow shoot. Wulf pointed towards a giant willow standing massive and alone at the far end of the clearing, its leaf-laden branches climbing above the roots thickly carpeted with columbine and purple garlic.

'Wait here,' Wulf said, putting a hand on my arm.

He trotted down the meadow, jumped up to grasp the lowest branches, clung momentarily and then hauled himself into the body of the tree. The willow seemed to swallow him whole, his progress marked only by the rustling and trembling of foliage.

I stood alone in the glade. All around me elder and sweet-briar shrubs flaunted petals in colours softened by the filtered sunlight and breathed sweet fragrance from the flowers warmed by the summer air. Chaffinches flitted nervously from bush to bush, chattering to each other in harsh warning notes.

Willow branches rustled, bent and shuddered back into place as Wulf dropped lightly to the ground. Thrust through his belt like a riding whip was a long, leafy bough, presumably cut from high in the tree. He waved for me to join him under the willow. By the time I reached his side, he had already worked quickly and deftly with his knife to strip the bough of leaves; then he cut it into short staves, splitting each piece to reveal a flat side of freshly cut wood backed by a bark-covered, curved edge. He bevelled one end of the first stave, then cut a split into it.

'This is the mouth,' he said, shaping it carefully. 'The runes will speak to the spirits through it.'

When he had cut a number of staves in the same fashion, he collected them into a neat pile. There were at least a dozen of them.

'Now watch closely. I want you to carve into these sticks the symbols I am cutting.'

He selected a stave and placed it on the ground, flat side facing up, then held it fast with his feet, one on either end. Holding his knife lightly in his palm, as if to throw the weapon, he cut into the wood with the point. He handled the knife with exquisite balance and accuracy and the runes were carved clearly and deeply. When he had finished he picked up the sliver, brushed and blew wood shavings from it and handed it to me. He had carved four rune-shapes very close together.

'What does it mean, Wulf?'

'It is a message to the spirit-world, telling them who you are and why you are here.'

'Don't they already know?'

Wulf smiled, but his eyes remained serious. 'It is advisable for you to have the message on your person. You may encounter spirits who do not wish to welcome you.'

He pointed a finger towards the freshly cut staves of willow, cutting off further questions.

'Copy these runes onto the sticks.'

I selected a sliver of willow, placed it on the ground and squatted over it with my feet on either end, as Wulf had done. Slipping my knife from its sheath, I began to copy his shapes but immediately ran into difficulty. It was virtually impossible to control the length of the lines and the cuts were of wildly uneven depth. When I had completed the first stave, Wulf picked it up to inspect my work: it was a mess.

He made no comment, but passed me another sliver and I prepared to start again.

'Wait,' Wulf said, grasping my wrist. 'Study the wood first. You must get to know the flow of the grain. The pattern of wyrd represented by this tree is visible in the grain and you must work within it.'

My first attempt had been so crude that I doubted whether knowledge of the grain would make any difference, but I made a show of looking carefully at the exposed side of the stave.

'It is important,' Wulf insisted, as if reading my thoughts. 'A straight cut into one piece of wood will be curved or angled in another piece, because of the different pattern of grain. And you must remember that you are cutting runes into wood, so that they have depth as well as shape. The flow of grain is important in keeping an even depth.'

I placed the willow stave on the ground and began working again. This time I held the knife blade at a slight angle, so that I could see more clearly the cuts I was making, and I tried to allow for the direction of the grain. My cuts were more sure and direct at first, but then my second rune-shape went hopelessly wrong and I started to carve over it to correct the mistake. Again Wulf stopped me by grasping my wrist.

'The wood grain will exaggerate your errors if you try to correct what you have done. It is better to continue. Do not worry about mistakes. More important is that your rune-carvings express naturally what you are trying to say, rather than conforming to some standard of appearance.'

'But Wulf, I do not know what I am trying to say. I can carve the shapes, but I still do not know exactly what these inscriptions mean. I am trying to copy your runes, for they are the only ones I have worked with – surely the important thing is for my runes to resemble yours as closely as possible?'

Wulf shook his head emphatically.

'Each sorcerer has his own connections with the forces of wyrd. In the execution of the shapes subtleties, allusions and personal secrets are revealed. Once you have mastered the copying skill, you will develop your own style and in time your knife will dance in your hand. But no matter how elegant your runes become, they will never be a truer expression of your nature than they are now.'

I continued working under Wulf's supervision, beginning a new willow sliver as soon as I had finished the previous one. The work seemed crude and ugly in comparison with quill and vellum scripting at the monastery. I thought of the illuminated sheets that were prepared in the scriptorium, in each of which we could recognise the work of individuals expressed in the pull of the quill, roundness of figures and detail of decoration. But they were each artist's unique celebration of the Lord, in contrast with which these inelegant carvings in wood seemed to require nothing more than mechanical skill.

Eventually I had carved on all of the sticks except one, and on the whole each effort produced a more accurate replica of Wulf's runes than had the preceding stave. By the standards of my first rune-stave, I was pleased with the improvement. I stretched and stood up slowly. Wulf picked up the last stave I had carved, examined it and grunted non-committally, but I could tell by his eyes that he was impressed and pleased by my efforts. He looked up at me and caught me watching him.

'You have done well,' he admitted, smiling.

I blushed quickly, suddenly aware that I had been seeking a compliment. Now that I had received it, I felt ashamed that I had wanted it. I thought immediately of Eappa and how I used to show him my lettering in as casual a manner as possible, but full of hope for a word of praise. And every time Eappa encouraged me, I knew that he had seen through my carefully concealed pride.

I bent again to complete my task, but Wulf stopped me. 'Here. Use this for the last stave.'

I stared at the handle of his knife, then back at his face.

'It is better suited than yours for the cutting of runes and this last stave is important.'

I took the knife. Despite its large size, it balanced beautifully in my hand and the feel of the haft made my palm tingle. Carefully, I cut one final series of runes and Wulf picked up the stave and examined it closely. Then he took back his knife and carefully shaved very thin strips of wood several inches down from the top, but leaving them attached to the stave. He did this all the way around the willow stick and then, gripping between the side of his blade and his thumb, he pulled the knife repeatedly along each shaving until it curled over. When he had finished, the stave looked as if it had a mass of curly hair at the end.

Finally Wulf cut a slit a short distance from the curly end and a round circle half-way down.

'These are the mouth and the heart,' he explained, handing the bizarre piece of wood to me. 'Always carry this stave on your body. It will protect you from the spirits. They will not harm you intentionally, Brand, but you must retain this rune-stick until you feel absolutely ready to face the spirits on their own terms.'

I nodded my understanding, but in my heart I did not believe it. I did not see how a carved stick, lacking the blessing of the Lord, could carry with it the protection afforded by my crucifix. When Wulf turned away to tie his knife back into its sheath, I fingered the outline of my crucifix, solid and strong next to my skin. Carelessly, I slipped the small, lightweight rune-stick inside my tunic where it would remain safely trapped by my belt.

Wulf collected up the small heap of rune-staves on which I had practised carving. One by one, he snapped the staves in half, then dug a shallow hole in the ground and buried them.

'Wulf, I heard all you have told me about wyrd and omens and runes. But I still do not understand how all this leads you to think you can predict the death of a warrior from the flight of the ravens.'

Wulf said nothing, busily scraping leaves and loose vegetation over the covered hole in which he had buried the broken rune-staves. I feared that I had offended him and was trying to find a way of placating him when he suddenly stood up and started to whistle in a strange but melodic fashion. Almost at once, I recognised a convincing mimicry of the song of a blackbird. Wulf watched me quizzically, blond eyebrows raised, eyes twinkling with humour.

'The birds speak to me as surely and clearly as you do,' he said. 'Their songs are like incantations from the spells of wyrd.'

He resumed his inane whistling. At that moment I heard a

rustling sound behind me and turned just on time to see the glossy blur of a blackbird launching into flight from a shrub; it passed directly over us and with a wet splash a lump of bird droppings streaked onto my tunic. Wulf collapsed with laughter.

'If you understand the omens of birds, you would have realised what the bird was going to do.'

His shoulders bobbed up and down – laughter bubbling out of him, spilling around the clearing and bouncing back from the trees. I felt a sudden thrill of companionship, an almost tangible warmth between us. I felt as if, long ago in some other existence, we had sat together in a forest clearing and laughed until we cried.

'Come on,' Wulf chuckled, slapping my arm playfully. 'We have no more time for talk of runes and ravens.'

Quickly cleaning my tunic with grass, I collected up my sack, bag and cloak and, with a final glance down river towards the spot where the ravens had disappeared, I followed Wulf back into the forest shadows.

6

LIVING LIKE A WARRIOR

THE SETTING sun sat on distant hilltops like an orange-painted shield and the afternoon light began to fade. Wulf stopped on a ridge and pointed to a thickly wooded valley below, lying sea green in the descending dusk. I followed the direction of his arm and saw grey fire-smoke drifting in the wind above the trees, half-way up the opposite slope. Beneath the smoke, in a small area cleared of trees, sat a large timber hall surrounded by a stockade, with houses and huts spilling down the hill towards a stream at the base of the valley.

We set off downhill towards the settlement, and when it dropped out of sight behind the trees we followed the plumes of smoke rising above the treeline like beacons. Dense stands of beech and birch opened into fields cleared for ploughing and eventually into a meadow which sloped up towards the large hall dominating the skyline. As soon as we entered the meadow I heard a dog bark and looked nervously at Wulf; in my homeland a traveller leaving the road either shouts or blows a horn, lest he may be regarded as a thief to be killed or ransomed.

Several figures emerged from the shelter of the buildings, stood stock-still in the shadows watching our approach and then yelled something back into the compound. To my consternation a dozen or more men came out of the gate and hurried down the meadow towards us. But far from being hostile, they approached Wulf with deference, ducking their heads and grinning like nervous dogs. A small detachment of children ran towards us, looking expectantly into Wulf's face; suddenly one of them darted forward, touched his tunic and then dashed off, laughing and shouting with the others. Two women joined the throng and presented Wulf with an armful of dyed linen, apparently as a gift. Throughout all the excitement Wulf behaved almost regally, as if he had expected such a welcome. The whole scene was confusing to me; I could not fathom the significance Wulf held for the people of the settlement.

Suddenly, I noticed several people eyeing me suspiciously, and I realised that I would have to reveal my status as an observer of their customs and beliefs. I cursed myself for not having worked out a false identity with Wulf.

Wulf turned towards me. 'This is Wat Brand,' he announced. 'A friend. He journeys with me.'

The perfunctory introduction seemed to result in immediate acceptance of my presence: men shook me by the hand, their eyes shy and guarded and it was clear from their demeanour that I was being accorded high status as Wulf's companion.

We were led up the meadow, past houses and huts and into the compound of the main hall, surrounded by a timber-stake stockade. Two goats tethered in the lee of a building stopped eating, looked up with interest and then resumed their busy munching. Clucking chickens scattered as we walked across the compound to a house adjacent to the main hall; it had a good, steep thatch and a sturdy timber weather-porch protecting the entrance. Wulf and I were ushered into the house, the door latched behind us and the excited chatter of people outside gradually faded into the distance.

The one-room house was cool and dark, save for chinks of evening grey-light filtering through the smoke-hole in the roof and gaps around the door. Down either side of the room, against the two longest walls, ran raised benches topped with linen-covered mattresses, and the centre of the room was taken up by a raised fire-pit, raked clean and laid with fresh kindling. The planked floor was strewn with dried rushes and aromatic, creamy-flowered meadowsweet. Without doubt it was a guest-house, carefully prepared as if in anticipation of an important visitor.

I dropped my bag and sat heavily on one of the beds, feeling exhausted. Wulf hung his cloak and bag from wooden pegs set into the oak cross-beam.

'Wulf, why are these people afraid of you?'

'What do you mean?' he said, his innocent expression just too exaggerated to be convincing.

'This house has been prepared for your arrival, they have given you presents and they speak to you with deference and respect. And yet I saw them watching you out of the corners of their eyes—they are afraid of you.'

He shrugged his shoulders. 'I have been of service to them in the past. As a consequence they are pleased to welcome me.'

'But why are they afraid of you?' I persisted. I felt that it was important for me to establish the basis for Wulf's status in the settlement.

'The people pay me for each task that I perform for them,' he said softly. 'But they also bestow gifts at the beginning and end of my season of travel. They believe that if I were not treated properly, then I could bring great misfortune to them.'

He looked up at me, his white teeth bared in a sudden, broad grin. 'They are right,' he said, chuckling. I felt a shiver of apprehension in the pit of my stomach; beneath his warm and easy exterior lurked darker depths as yet unknown to me.

Wulf stood and walked to the door. 'I have business to attend to. You can rest here for a while. They will give us food later.'

He opened the door and latched it quietly behind him as he left. Alone in the room, I sank back gratefully on to the mattress. Without moving from the bed, I unstrapped the bandage and leaves from my ankle and dropped them on the floor. The swelling had completely subsided and the ankle gave no pain at all. I tried to think through all I had experienced with Wulf, but I had not slept properly for two nights and drowsiness slowed my thoughts. I closed my eyes and slipped into slumber.

*   *   *

I awoke with a start and peered around the candlelit room. Someone was shaking me by the arm.

'Wake up!' a voice said loudly. 'It's midnight. The thanes are having a hunting feast and we are guests.'

I looked at Wulf in surprise; I had expected the familiar face of the sub-prior, touring the dormitory with lighted lantern to awaken late sleepers for prayers.

'Is everybody going?' I mumbled, groping for my shoes.

'Warriors only – and us,' he replied, creaking open the door.

I clutched my cloak and, still warm with sleep, followed Wulf
through the darkness to the main hall, looming two-storeyed into
the night sky. Horses snorted and stamped in nearby stables and
through the open door of a work hut I saw saddles and harness
leather being cleaned under the light of oil lamps. The warriors
must have ridden into the settlement while I slept.

Guards at the entrance to the hall took little notice of us as we
crossed the cobbled threshold into the massive room. The air
hung heavy with the odour of mutton-fat candles, wood-smoke
and roasting meat spitted over roaring log fires set in trenches
down the centre of the hall. Side benches were fronted with
boarded trestles and we crowded in at the lower end of a long
trestle already full of men.

I counted at least forty men in the hall, though I recognised
only two of the faces I had seen earlier in the day. Then, my eyes
still smarting from wood-smoke, I looked around the hall. It was
magnificent: at least twenty paces long and perhaps half as wide,
with blazing torches in wall brackets arcing great shadow shapes
up into the high, smoke-blackened roof-beams. Massive support-
ing timbers, strengthened with iron clamps, were graven and
painted with boars and serpents writhing in the flickering
firelight, and behind the benches stretched enormous tapestried
wall-hangings; skins, horns, shields and swords glittered in wall-
hung racks. I had never been in such a splendid building.

'There sits the power in this part of the kingdom,' Wulf
whispered in my ear, gesturing towards the raised platform at the
north wall. It was packed with older thanes and dominated by a
huge, magnificently carved and decorated chair.

'Cydda has yet to make his entrance,' he continued. 'He rode
in this night with twenty thanes and will leave tomorrow. He has
six halls in this forest alone and is hoping for greater gifts yet
from the King.'

Suddenly benches and trestles scraped as people scrambled to
their feet and a thane who could only have been Cydda strode
majestically into the hall, accompanied by a clanking group of
bodyguards. He was a big, broad-chested warrior, with long, fine
blue cloak swept back at his left hip to reveal a glittering, jewel-

encrusted sword-hilt. He took his place in the enormous chair, firelight flaring off his gold headband and arm-rings. The thanes sat down again.

As soon as Cydda was seated, the large, black cooking pot suspended above the fire was winched noisily to the ground. Slaves with cropped hair and collars pulled racks of spitted fowl from the flames and chopped them on to trenchers, while two bakers carried boards of steaming bread and cakes which were removed with tongs and placed carefully on the trenchers. More meat was heaped on to side tables of upturned shields, the aroma of roasted venison gradually camouflaging other smells. Leather pitchers of ale and mead were pushed along the tables.

I was overwhelmed by the sheer splendour of the feast and my mouth ran wet at the sight of the food. But I could not eat; it seemed to me sacrilege that I should feast in a place of such pagan ostentation. I watched hungry mouths tearing at the hot meat, and an image formed in my mind of the ragged packs of peasants who had trudged pathetically into the monastery the previous winter; hollow-eyed people, with wailing children, begging for food. The previous summer had yielded a miserable harvest and winter wrought near famine throughout the Mercian kingdom. Yet the monastery gardens had provided sufficient and the monks had preached that the famine was the Lord's punishment for sins. I remembered Brother Eappa's prediction: 'When the peasants are hungry, they are weak in flesh and in spirit. By midwinter they will be scrambling for crumbs of comfort from their heathen gods.' After hearing Eappa's words I prayed fervently for the souls of the peasants and for their faith to be strengthened, but sadly Eappa was right. Their faith did not sustain them. Rather than asking for the Lord's forgiveness, the peasants resorted to bribing devils and our chapel had again become empty.

Wulf pushed a trencher of meat in front of me.

'Fasting at a feast will arouse suspicions,' he said, nodding encouragingly towards the plate.

He was right – my mission would not be helped by self-indulgent martyrdom. Breathing a silent prayer, I picked up the food. As soon as I started to eat I realised that I was ravenous; I ate and drank heavily and soon the wine made my ears hum.

Wulf ate slowly, though he seemed to be enjoying the occasion.

'Listen carefully to the speeches,' he said, his eyes crinkling with amusement. With concentration I could follow the alien dialects, as one by one the thanes climbed to their feet to fawn upon Cydda with spendid flights of oratory and glowing accounts of his deeds of valour. Cydda grinned broadly, though his smile never reached his bright, pig-like, intelligent eyes and he dispensed gold rings and bracelets like a man training hunting hawks.

Suddenly, at the height of the celebrations, Wulf stood as if to leave. I swung my legs over the bench and reached to pull my cloak from the beam-hooks behind me.

'Stay!' Wulf said firmly.

I looked at him in surprise. 'Stay here,' he repeated, buckling on his cloak. Then he leaned over and spoke into my ear, though no one could overhear amidst the general uproar.

'You must stay and observe closely if you wish to know the ways of our people.'

I looked into his face and he winked broadly; his expression was warm and friendly, but his eyes betrayed the cunning of a fox.

Before I could protest, Wulf stepped lightly across the hall, a guard leaned heavily on one of the huge doors and my guide slipped out into the darkness.

I settled back on to the bench in puzzlement. I could recall nothing that could have precipitated his departure and he had not told me what to watch for. I concentrated again on the speeches, thinking that Wulf might have recognised an orator who would tell stories of their gods.

Suddenly, without warning, I was toppled backwards from the bench as thanes all around me jumped to their feet and, as I recovered my footing, I was swept along by the crowd and pushed on to a serving bench with others, all scrambling for a clearer view of Cydda's table. Voices bellowed belligerently above the general commotion and I could see Cydda standing impassively, thick arms folded across his chest, as a dozen or more men heaved his heavy table to the side of the hall. Near the kitchen door I caught sight of two warriors stripping off their tunics. The drunken atmosphere throbbed with excitement and I was struck with a sickening sense of foreboding; Brother Eappa condemned challenge matches between warriors. Indeed, the Christian King of Mercia had been persuaded to increase wergild, so that a man who kills has to pay such heavy compensation to the dead man's family that the thanes no longer consider fights a worthwhile adventure. I would have left immediately, but for Wulf's admonition to stay.

Around me thanes weaved about trying to obtain a clearer view, shouting encouragement and abuse as the two warriors materialised in the cleared space, each gripping a sword in his right hand and a light, brightly coloured round shield in his left. The two men circled each other warily, shield-bosses gleaming in the firelight, carefully placed feet scuffing through the floor-straw. One of them faced directly towards me. He was clearly younger than his opponent, with large eyes and short blond hair, his knuckles white on the sword-hilt. Suddenly he whipped his sword through the air at knee height and with a sense of revulsion I expected to see his opponent's legs cut from under him. Incredibly the older man leapt high, his tucked legs clearing the swinging sword blade while the attacker, thrown off balance by his failure to connect, spun through the crowd and crashed into the wall. A dislodged tapestry flopped into a dusty heap by his side.

Shouts and jeers rang in my ears. My heart pounded like a hammer and my tongue was dry as leather.

The young warrior heaved himself away from the wall and back into battle. His older opponent made no move to attack but stood still, peering through slitted eyes, his jaw clamped with concentration and his breath sucking deeply and noisily through his nose. His lean, lined face betrayed no emotion as he deftly altered his leather shield-grip so that it was strapped around his left forearm and clasped his sword in both hands, twirling it softly in front of him. Swiftly he stepped forward and swung sideways at his opponent's body, then at the last moment changed the direction of his blow; the blade arced upward towards the dark rafters and swept down hard. The younger fighter anticipated this and the powerful blow cut deeply into his raised wooden shield. The big swordsman wrenched his weapon free, showering shield splinters into the fire.

I swallowed hard, trying to control the feeling of nausea that had gripped my stomach, and stared unblinking as they circled again, their breath rasping and hissing. The smaller man struck once more; whirled his sword above his head and swung it down, swivelled his wrists and sliced the blade directly at his opponent's neck. The older thane met the blow with his shield and the sword carved into it and locked. Frantically the young warrior tried to jerk his sword free; I caught a glimpse of his eyes, wide and panic-stricken like those of a trapped rabbit. In that instant the big man's sword again arced overhead and hurtled downward. The smaller warrior crouched under his useless sword and moved close to his opponent, inside the swing of the sword-blade, but the heavy hand-guard of the weapon cracked against the side of his head and he swerved across the room in a blind stagger, hit his head against a wall timber with a sickening thud and fell into a soft, crumpled heap. His head spilled crimson on the floor-straw.

With a tremendous roar the thanes surged around the victor, hoisted him to their shoulders and carried him around the hall. I stood alone on the table, with a clear view of the fallen man; he lay absolutely still, skull gleaming whitely through blood-soaked flesh, body twisted unnaturally, eyes staring blankly. My knees trembled and I felt sick. Slowly I climbed from the table, walked unsteadily across the hall to collect my cloak and made my way to the door. The guards had left their posts to join the others in toasting the health of the victor and I stood alone, unnoticed, an outsider in the shadows. I pushed hard against the heavy door; it groaned ajar and I slipped out into the cool night air. A fresh breeze cleared my head and I breathed the sweet scent of a summer night as I hurried through the deserted compound, still dazed and shocked; I had seen people die of age and sickness, but never had I witnessed a life snatched away in a drunken brawl.

Reaching the porch of the guest-house, I turned back to look at the hall, shrouded in darkness. The sounds of celebration drifted faintly from the building and I could hear the stamping and snorting of tethered horses, nervous in unfamiliar stables. Suddenly my eye caught movement on the roof of the hall. I scanned the roof-line and eaves, barely discernible against the dark night sky. Then I saw something that caught my breath:

two ravens were perched on the roof near the smoke-hole, their black silhouettes motionless. I remembered Wulf's horrific prediction and with a shudder I turned quickly, entered the house and slammed the door shut behind me.

A low fire glowed in the fire-pit. I stared through the gloom; Wulf's bed was empty. I sat on my bed, leaned forward and warmed my hands in front of the fire. I was not cold, but my legs still trembled with fear and the warmth of the fire was comforting. At first I was obsessed by the image of the ravens but eventually, as time passed, I was able to dismiss their appearance as a coincidence. There were many ravens in the forest and two on the roof of the hall were no more significant than the pair we had seen at the river.

I stretched out on my mattress. I was not sleepy, but my head reeled with wine-glow. I suddenly felt very depressed and frightened and hopelessly inadequate for the Mission with which I had been entrusted; the events in the hall had shaken me badly and I just did not know how many more such experiences I could stomach.

Suddenly the door latch clacked open, the low fire jumped and swirled in the sudden draught and Wulf stepped into the room. He closed the door, squatted in front of the fire and stirred the embers; in the light of the awakening flames I could see him regarding me intently.

'Why did you do that?' I hissed, sitting up and swinging my feet to the floor. 'Why did you leave me to witness such barbarity? A man was killed over there.'

Wulf sat on his bed and looked at me steadily.

'I thought you wished to learn about our ways,' he said, his voice almost a whisper.

'Your gods and customs, not your brawls,' I protested angrily.

'I am sorry if it upset you,' he said gently, 'but such things happen.'

'You make the process of killing sound natural!' I retorted. 'How can the smashed skull of a warrior be dismissed so lightly?'

'Surely warriors wield swords in your homeland, Brand?'

'When men come to God there will be no more killing,' I said, trembling with anger.

Wulf snorted in derision. 'The warrior kings will use your god as an addition to their sword power. He will become another justification for their military exploits. Warriors are people who choose to live by the sword; they wager their lives against the odds of losing it, in exchange for the golden gifts of a warlord. They are ruled by the destiny of death.'

He leaned across the fire-pit towards me, his expression softening.

'I am not condoning that kind of violence,' he said softly, 'but you fail to understand. What I want to tell you is that death stalks us constantly and eventually will claim us all. The one thing we can be sure of is that we are bound to die. Life and death are the summer and winter of Middle-Earth. One is not possible without the other, for a perpetual summer would burn up Middle-Earth like a funeral pyre; a perpetual winter would return it to the grip of the Frost Giants.'

I was too upset by the grisly murder to listen meekly to Wulf's heathen homilies. 'Our death is in the hands of the Lord,' I protested resolutely. 'Our life on this Earth is but a preparation for the call of the Lord.'

Wulf shook his head slowly. 'The secrets of life and death are different for the sorcerer. The patterns of wyrd far exceed the tiny horizons of the ordinary person, for he is capable of seeing only short spans of time. Your eyes break up the course of life into tiny segments and label them as separate entities. The eyes of a sorcerer do not have this false focus. Life is comprised of waterfalls, rapids, eddies and whirlpools, but they are all part of the same watercourse. For me, life and death flow together as aspects of one river. For you, life is like a series of unconnected rain puddles and death comes when the sun dries them all up.'

He was wrong, of course, for he knew nothing of our belief in the Heavenly Kingdom. But he was neatly sidestepping the important issues with shields of images.

'But Wulf, what has your view of life and death to do with a warrior being hacked to pieces? Surely he had many more winters and summers to live?'

Wulf shrugged again, as if there were no issue to answer.

'Both warriors who fought in the hall had probably accepted the inevitability of death before they even stripped for combat. The finest warriors use death as a resource, for they must live with their wits all the time, whereas for most people life is based on the assumption that they will live to an old age. With the illusion of time to spare, their lives lack urgency, intensity. A life of fantasy takes over like a fungus. Thoughts become clouded with images of future events and the actions and emotions of the moment are postponed indefinitely. The warrior must accept, deep within his heart, that one day he will be dead and that day could be today. The greatest fighters live as an arrow, not a target. The arrow speeds through space cleanly, swiftly, directly; alive and moving, it has direction and an end point, but in between it soars. The target merely stays still, waiting for something to happen.'

Wulf stopped talking just long enough to ensure that I was still listening.

'For the sorcerer, also, death is a resource, for living with wyrd takes us to the limit. Your life, in which avoidance of death is paramount, means that you live constantly within your capabilities, for to push to the limits is to risk death. But the sorcerer has to accept his own death, because when he approaches the spirits he is like a moth heading for fire-flames.'

I laughed nervously. Talk of death always made me feel uneasy, even physically weak. But Wulf's views were so alien, dark and disturbing that I did not wish to deal with them. I reached for the comfort of my faith:

'I am listening to all you are saying, Wulf, but it is impossible for me to understand because my faith is so very different. We believe that when God's hand is laid upon us, then He is calling us to follow Him into the Heavenly Kingdom. The body and soul part and the soul enters heaven as spirit. But it is not for us to determine when and how this blessed event should take place.'

Wulf smiled suddenly, quickly and nodded in agreement.

'We too believe in the presence of soul and its disappearance at death.'

For a moment I was stunned – Eappa had not prepared me for this.

'How is that so, Wulf? I thought you denied the existence of the soul?'

'You have been ill-informed,' he said, chuckling cheerfully. 'Within each person, three forces surge like three streams converging on a whirlpool. These forces are the life-force, soul and shield-skin. Life-force I have told you about. The soul is the essence of wyrd, present in everything. It is the very being of which we are formed. The soul is what gives form, direction and pattern to all things, for it forms a shield-skin around the life-force, enveloping vitality in a recognisable shape. The form of the shield-skin defines the kind of creature we are. The shield must be continually maintained with each succeeding breath, for if it is not then life-force would burst from it like molten metal, shapeless, uncontrollably leaking back into the earth. The soul is the essence and at the moment of death, when the shield-skin ceases and life-force returns to the Mother Earth, the soul leaves the body and leads an existence separate from it.'

My mind whirled, trying to grasp these concepts together. I was particularly fascinated by his view of the soul, for there Eappa's interest would be most surely gripped.

Wulf leaned back on one elbow, thoughtfully staring into the fire.

'Whatever has no soul, does not exist in Middle-Earth, for without a soul there can be no concentration of life-force and no shield-skin to envelop it. That is why everything you can see in Middle-Earth has soul.'

I nodded knowingly; I now remembered that Eappa had taught me that the pagans ascribed spiritual power to every manner of creature. But this mistake was as nothing compared with the monstrous error of claiming that soul was present in everything. Only man has soul, for only man is Divinely Blessed and created in His image.

'How can you believe that soul is present in everything, Wulf?' I said gently, afraid that criticism might discourage his talkative mood.

Wulf sat up and spread his hands, palms upwards, in a gesture of futility as if being asked to explain the obvious.

'It is apparent that the soul is present in everything observable in Middle-Earth, for the soul continually breathes out the shield-skin which strikes your eye. Without it, the object would be invisible and therefore have no soul.'

Smiling to myself, I leaned forward and pointed to one of the large rocks which formed a fender encircling the fire-pit.

'Rocks do not breathe, Wulf. Surely then, they cannot have soul?'

Wulf watched me steadily, through narrowed eyes. 'Rocks breathe,' he said evenly. 'But each breath lasts longer than life and death for a man. Hills and mountains breathe, but each breath lasts a thousand human lifetimes.'

There was no possible reply to this assertion and I leaned back in satisfaction. The terrible event in the mead-hall was at least yielding invaluable information. As before, I was impressed by Wulf's sincerity and conviction but abhorred the comprehensive errors of his beliefs. Chuckling to myself, I pictured Eappa's incredulous expression when I told him that pagan rocks have souls.

Suddenly Wulf threw back his head and bayed with laughter so raucous that I practically jumped from my bed with alarm. He doubled up, cackling and hooting, and I soon began to feel angry for I had no idea what he was laughing at.

'You do not, do not . . .' he gurgled, waving a hand helplessly towards me. 'You do not believe a word of this, do you?'

I smiled back coldly. I could not see the humour.

The fire leaped and spluttered as another piece of wood collapsed into the flames. Wulf's laughter subsided as quickly as it had arisen.

'All right,' he said, nodding to himself. 'All right! I shall tell you something you can believe.'

He fixed me with a look that chilled me to the core, his eyes clouding over strangely so that his pupils seemed enormous. Then he spoke:

'At this very moment, I could tell you when you will die, where you will die and how you will die. Would you like me to tell you?'

My throat went dry. I did not believe him, for no man can have such knowledge of God's will. But I could not hold his gaze and dropped my eyes.

'If you do not believe me, then the information will mean nothing to you,' he said coolly. 'So there is no harm in my telling you the circumstances of your death.'

He spoke with sureness and conviction, yet I knew that he was attempting to bully me into submission, frustrated because I was not instantly converted to his vision of death. It was a cheap ploy and I had every right to call his bluff.

But he sat and gazed at me with eyes like slits and I realised with awesome certainty that he knew about my death: he had foreseen it.

Wulf opened his mouth to speak.

'No!' I gasped, reaching out a hand as if to stop him. 'No, I do not want to know.'

He regarded me for a moment. 'Very few people wish to be given that information,' he said at last.

I felt ashamed, horrified at what I had done. My legs still trembled with fear.

Wulf leaned forward and spoke almost in a whisper. 'To encounter the spirits and enter their world, the sorcerer enters the realms of his own death. The soul is like a shadow and the sorcerer is able to detach the soul from the body and journey amongst spirits. You will have to do the same.'

The fire spluttered and then crackled into life as a fresh piece of firewood succumbed to the flames. I watched it open-mouthed, paralysed by the impossibility of Wulf's claim. I did not want to pursue it; I desperately wanted Wulf to turn the conversation away from the darkness of my own death.

'Death as a resource seems a long way from the murder of the warrior, Wulf.'

My voice sounded small and far away. I drew my knees up into my chest, dreading another statement directed at the ending of my life.

Mercifully, Wulf sat back and shifted the focus of the discussion.

'As I told you, the greatest mistake we can make is to become attached to our shield-skin and to treat it as something we wish to preserve for ever,' he said, suddenly cheerful as if he were discussing a change in the weather. 'Trying to preserve the shield-skin merely dams up the flow of life-force. The shield-skin is a temporary existence; life-force flows like a stream and the shield-skin should be the valley through which it flows, not a stagnant pool blocking its movement.

'As I have told you, the mightiest warriors use death as a resource. And yet their enemies often do not realise the resources of a warrior until it is too late. I knew a brave and noble warrior who lived very near this settlement. He was no ordinary thane, drinking, boasting and fighting at every opportunity. Instead, he had come to terms with his death and therefore lived fully every instant of life.'

Wulf paused to crouch in front of the fire, adding more wood. Then he sat back on his bed and started telling his story, very quietly.

'This mighty warrior no longer fought for any army. Instead he lived on the edge of the forest, looking like any woodland dweller: brown and weather-beaten face, dressed in shaggy old skins. But he still had the special physical gifts of a great warrior. In particular, he had extraordinarily keen hearing; his ears were set high on his head and he could identify all the sounds of the forest by day or night. In fact, his only vulnerable area was his throat.'

Wulf made a cutting motion under his chin. 'He always kept his throat covered for protection and on the one occasion I saw it uncovered it was white, untouched by the sun. He lived a careful existence, for he had many enemies. He hunted for food at night and the few people who ever saw him say he ran swiftly, up on his toes.'

I was totally engrossed in the story already and relieved that the conversation had turned to lighter matters. I was impressed by the warrior; he sounded strange and fearsome and I reasoned that he must have lived in the woods because he had been exiled from a royal hall. I was about to ask Wulf, but he resumed the tale:

'He built a fortress into the side of a hill, where he lived with his family. Several times his enemies tracked him down to his hiding place and challenged him to come out and fight, but he never heeded them. Their haunts and threats did not lure him into battle, for while he stayed in his stronghold he was particularly impervious to attack. Once his chief rivals even broke into the main part of his fortress with trained hounds to catch him, but he escaped along secret tunnels cut into the hill behind his dwelling and emerged from them safely on to the hillside.

'His retreat convinced his enemies that he was a coward. They reasoned that if they could catch him by surprise and unarmed, they might be able to follow him to his stronghold and kill him with ease. This was a serious error.'

Wulf paused and cocked an eyebrow at me melodramatically. I was well and truly ensnared by his story-telling.

'One fateful night, his enemies lay in ambush, but somehow he knew they would be coming for him and he had prepared. They saw him tracking animals, apparently unarmed. He hurried back to his fortress with them in close pursuit and scurried off down one of his escape tunnels; they followed him, crawling on their bellies, staying close behind him right to the point where the tunnel emerged on to the hillside. Breathless, the warrior scrambled out on to the hill and his enemy closed in to attack. But the warrior had weapons at the ready and suddenly he whirled around and hurled scores of spears from close range, wounding his enemies terribly. He was deadly accurate. Never again was he attacked in the forest.'

Wulf chuckled with delight. Obviously the story had ended – a strange, heroic saga. Out of curiosity I asked Wulf the name of the warrior.

'The warrior was a hedgehog,' he replied, looking at me and waiting for my reaction. The expression on my face must have satisfied him, for he howled with laughter, I laughed with him. He had narrated the tale with consummate skill, full of drama and humour.

Still chuckling, Wulf heaped ash on to the fire to slow down the burning, then stretched out on his bed. I sat watching him through the darkness. He was a bewildering person: a man of mead-hall singers' word-hoard, of warmth and laughter which could turn to ice in a twinkling. He seemed happy to tell me of his beliefs and to spend hours trying to fashion images which would help me to understand. Yet he constantly hinted at dark and dangerous events to come, in which I would encounter the spirits at risk to my life. He attracted and repelled me at the same time; I liked him as a man, but was terrified of him as a sorcerer.

Suddenly, Wulf raised himself up on one elbow and looked over at me.

'There is something I forgot to tell you, Brand,' he said casually. 'The hedgehog was my guardian spirit and the enemies were trying to capture my soul. And they might have succeeded too, except for one thing – I was warned of their presence by the flight of ravens.'

7

TREMBLING THE WEB OF WYRD

DRUGGED AND dizzy with sleep, I crawled to the door and swung it ajar. Leather hinges creaked, fresh air swept through the open doorway and I collapsed back on to the mattress, my head reeling with the throb of last night's ale. From outside the shrill cries of an ox-herd pierced my ears and wooden-wheeled carts clattered and groaned as if they were driving through my skull. Then, in the distance, I heard the forge hammers ringing on metal like a clash of swords and the memory of last night's battle seeped into my memory, painful as a festering wound. I stared up into the smoke-blackened thatch of the guest-house, trying to shake my head clear of the nightmare images.

'Are you dead?' Wulf asked loudly, striding into the room and banging the door shut behind him.

He squatted next to my bed, reached inside his tunic, pulled out a small leather pouch, opened it and tipped two gold rings into his palm. He held them close to his face and examined them carefully in the dim light of the room. I struggled up on to one elbow and, still blinking sleep from my eyes, leaned over to look at them. They were fine rings and Wulf nodded slowly, apparently in satisfaction.

'I have been paid well,' he said. 'Come and watch me earn my treasure.'

He grasped his staff and one of the sacks that were piled next to his mattress and stood impatiently by the door. Hurriedly, I tied on my shoes and followed him out of the guest-house into the mid-morning light. I did not know what to expect, but the fact that Wulf had returned to the house to collect me suggested that he had something instructive to show me. As soon as we emerged from the timber porch, two men yoking oxen to a wattle-walled wagon left the animals and followed us. Our path cut between weaving huts and the clatter and clack of activity ceased as small groups of women hastened out to see where we were going. By the time we reached the western perimeter of the settlement the houses and work huts seemed to have emptied of people and we were surrounded by an eager crowd of onlookers.

The boundary of the farm's cleared land was marked by a fine stand of beech trees. Beneath them huddled a wattled enclosure and an adjacent timber stable, thatched roof sagging with age. At least a score of onlookers surged around the fence of the small paddock, but Wulf stood to one side, listening to the animated prattle of an angular, stick-thin man who was tugging nervously at the brim of a hat clutched tightly in his hands. Diffidently, I wandered over to join them.

'How many days?' Wulf was asking.

'Six days. At least six days.' The man looked imploringly at Wulf, watery eyes bulging from a florid face. 'If he dies, the master's wrath will . . . will . . .' His voice trailed away and he swallowed hard at the thought of his master discovering the horse to be dead.

Wulf stood, gazing impassively at the horse-keeper, seemingly unmoved by the urgency of the case. I began to feel sorry for the man; it was becoming clear to me that he had paid Wulf the two rings in exchange for some attempt to cure the sick horse, but I had no knowledge of what exactly Wulf was expected to do. Suddenly Wulf turned to me and winked ostentatiously.

'Come with me,' he said, tugging at my arm.

Wulf pushed through the crowd of people, hands patting and plucking at us as, reddening self-consciously, I followed him to the stable. The stable door creaked ajar on broken hinges and we climbed through a clutter of forks, rakes and other iron tools to emerge from the stable into the small enclosure. Wulf dropped his sack softly to the ground and propped his staff against the inside of the fence. About five paces distant, facing a rack of scythes and sickles, stood a handsome hunting horse, shaggy-maned and deep-chested. Above the buzzing chatter of the onlookers, I could hear the horse-keeper reciting the horse's symptoms repetitively to all within earshot. Wulf stood silently, watching the animal closely.

'Look at his belly,' Wulf said, turning to me.

The horse's stomach hung heavily and swollen.

'What else do you see?' he said suddenly, speaking loudly. I glanced at the faces crowding above the wattle fence and conversation died away as the people waited in silence for my observations. Blushing again, I swept my eyes over the horse, seeking signs of anything unusual.

'His flanks are wet,' I said. 'And his mouth bubbles with foam.'

I thought I had stated the obvious but Wulf seemed satisfied.

The horse turned his head slowly towards us and shuffled closer to the stable, deeper into the shade of the stable-roof. Mucus hung in a long stream from his flared nostrils and he looked very sick. Wulf padded over to his linen sack, pulled it open, dipped his cupped hands into it and brought out handfuls of a yellow, powdery substance. He approached the animal slowly, almost gliding towards him, making strange, soft, whistling sounds from the back of his throat. Then he pressed his palms to its muzzle, flicking his tongue in and out noisily. I thought at first that Wulf was attempting a cure with some specially prepared herbal or plant mixture, but then events changed dramatically. Still whistling softly, Wulf began to run his palms lightly and quickly over the entire body of the sweating horse, then he stopped and examined a particular spot on the horse's hide, apparently feeling for something with his fingers. To my amazement, his forefinger seemed to disappear into the horse's flesh. The animal trembled and rolled his eyes but otherwise did not move. I glanced quickly at the row of wide-eyed faces above the wattle fence; they were watching intently.

Taking a swift step back from the horse, Wulf whipped one hand inside his tunic and pulled out a large knife. It was not the knife with which he had carved runes, but another which I had not seen before. I stared at the knife with fascination; the end of the horn haft was deeply carved with shapes and symbols and three large brass nails hung on leather strips from the finger-guard. Lightly and softly Wulf moved in front of the horse and offered the animal a second handful of the dried plant mixture, held in his left palm. As the horse lowered its head to lick off the substance, quickly and decisively Wulf's right hand flashed out and cut a knife-mark deep into the horse's forehead. The large animal buckled slightly and staggered back half a step while I went cold with horror. For an instant I thought the animal had been killed by the blow, but the horse stood trembling, his eyes rolling. Wulf stalked around swiftly, cutting similar marks on each of the horse's legs. Blood welled into the slice of the blade but, strangely, did not run openly. Then he bobbed back in front of the animal's head, reached up high on the animal's forehead above the bright red cuts and apparently applied pressure. As the horse slowly lowered his head, Wulf gripped the animal's left ear with his left hand and with a sudden sharp twist of his knife-hand he cut a hole right through the ear. The horse trembled violently and whinnied and the crowd behind the fence stirred excitedly. Wulf bent the ear down, and peered into it as if he was trying to look through the knife-hole. The horse staggered sideways and turned slightly. Wulf hung on, apparently still staring into the animal's ear, but I could now see that his eyes were closed. Then he began to murmur in a low voice. I strained my ears to hear, but his chanting rapidly grew louder, into a strange, nasal, whining voice:

> Mighty horse of hel,
> Way-tamer of wyrd,
> Winged steed of Woden,
> Star-stallion, bearer of secrets,
> Amble, trot, canter and gallop,
> Summoned by Middle-Earth spells.
> Let me hear your tread,
> Return these spirits to the land of the dead.

He repeated the refrain twice more, like a private prayer, and the sound had a strange effect on me. The atmosphere in the small enclosure felt heavy and oppressive and I had difficulty in breathing. My back ran with sweat.

Abruptly, Wulf stopped singing, stepped away from the horse, strode towards me and reached for his long staff which he had propped against the fence. As he turned back towards the horse I glimpsed his eyes. They burned with an eerie intensity, like emeralds and immediately I felt a sensation as if a cold breeze had cut across the back of my neck and someone had pulled my head forward. Wulf padded back to the animal and my head jerked upright, feeling airy and light as a feather. I shook my head vigorously to clear it, but I could not rid myself of a disturbing dizziness.

Wulf raised his staff high above his head, held it there for an instant, then with a chilling shriek he cracked the wooden shaft down hard on the horse's back. Immediately the horse bolted in a frenzied canter around the small enclosure, his head rising and plunging. Wulf bounded over the fence and I scrambled after him, tearing my tunic on the hazel hurdles. The crowd of onlookers burst into life, laughing and clapping, and the horse-keeper gripped Wulf's hand emotionally, tears brimming in his eyes.

I glanced back at the horse suspiciously. As I watched, the animal gradually slowed down and eventually ambled to the corner of the enclosure, pulling calmly at a small pile of hay. He gleamed with sweat and his stomach still appeared swollen, but his demeanour had altered entirely; he no longer breathed in wheezing gasps, his rigid stance had disappeared and he was eating readily.

'The horse was elf-shot,' Wulf announced loudly, the faces crowding around him shiny-eyed and admiring. 'Pierced all over with elves' arrows. The animal's life-force was leaking out through the arrow-holes like a rotten water barrel. My power-plant mixture restored the life-force of the animal while I did battle with the elves.'

I tried to conceal my embarrassment and disappointment; in Mercia, elves were figures of common superstition among the peasants and condemned as devils by the monks. I felt sure that there must be a worthier explanation to account for Wulf's astonishing feat of healing.

'I could hardly see him for arrow-holes,' he went on. 'I could feel the holes where the arrows penetrated his hide, and indentations made by arrows that bounced off him.'

'You could feel the holes with your fingers?' someone asked, excitedly.

'Yes,' he said. 'Then I cut rune symbols of power around the horse's flanks so that the horse would not be vulnerable to a fresh attack by elves. There is no point in healing an animal if it is immediately vulnerable to another attack. Then I cut a power-ring in the horse's ear, to give me entry into the inside of the horse where I attacked the elves, with help from the horse's guardian spirit. I attacked them with a look of power. My look weakened their grip on the horse and I immediately hit the animal with my staff and all the elves' arrows fell out.'

Wulf peered over at me to gauge my reaction, a broad smile creeping across his face.

I thought his explanation was preposterous. He began to chuckle. 'Elves are small,' he continued, smiling, indicating with his hand a height of about one foot. 'An elf is as much short of human size as a giant towers above it.' It was clear to everyone that Wulf was now talking for my benefit and eyes turned on me. 'There are different kinds of elves: light elves and dark elves, for example. Light elves are slender and slight. They appear beautiful to us. The dark elves, on the other hand, are ill-shaped, with coarse clothing, and appear ugly. The light elves are associated with the realms of the gods, but that does not mean you can always trust them. If you approach them wrongly they will behave like dark elves. In fact, even when you know the elves intimately, it is often difficult to tell at first what kind you are dealing with. The dark elves are by far the most dangerous; they even masquerade as pale elves to entrap you.'

Wulf seemed to be finding much amusement in his discourse and enjoying the rapt attention, but I felt nothing but an overwhelming sense of disappointment. I recognised the connections between Wulf's elves and the devils about which I had been warned by Eappa. He had told me of the evil creatures of pagan superstition who capture the souls of ignorant people in opposition to the Word of God, and I knew that Eappa would be pleased by my diligent reporting of Wulf's belief in elves. But I realised, with a sense of guilt, that I had hoped for something more from Wulf, for I could not reconcile my wonder at his healing powers with his description of devil-spirits as an explanation of his cure of the horse.

Still stunned by what I had seen, I walked back slowly towards the guest-house while Wulf remained at the stable amid the admiring throng. In a dreamy state I entered, sat on my mattress, leaned forward and buried my face in my hands. Carefully, deliberately, I pictured in my mind every detail of the procedures Wulf had followed in healing the horse. I knew that I had witnessed a display of healing power far outside my experience. And although I had heard tell of miraculous cures by the brethren, they were achieved by the grace of God: I did not know the source of Wulf's power, unless it be devils. But the stories of elves and invisible arrows, while obviously of use to the pagans in ordering the world of our Lord that was far beyond their understanding, nevertheless seemed pathetically primitive and unworthy of his abilities.

Yet again, I reviewed in my mind the procedures he had used. I began to think that the real secret of his cure must surely lie in the dried plant mixture he had fed to the horse, for I could not see how the power of devils could be used for such good purpose.

Then, in the soft light of the room, I saw piled against his bed four or five linen sacks, identical to the one from which he had taken the powder to give to the horse. I sat quietly for a moment, gathering my courage and my wits. Then stealthily I crawled to the doorway, pulled open the door and peered outside. The compound was deserted. I went across the porch and on to the path outside, looking towards the western perimeter of the settlement. In the distance I could see people drifting back in twos and threes towards the work-huts, chattering animatedly. I could not see Wulf amongst them and assumed that he was still at the stable.

Hurrying back into the house, I went straight to Wulf's side of the room and began to examine the largest sack. It had a heavily pungent odour. I patted the sack with my palms and could feel many different objects inside.

Next I tried another sack. This one was soft and crackled under my hands and felt as if it might be full of leaves and dried plants. Turning my attention to the top of the sack, I pulled gingerly at the tightly bound drawstring to loosen the knots.

Suddenly there was a sound behind me. I whirled around towards the doorway, but the door was still shut. My eyes swept the shadows along the floor, looking for a rat or mouse, but could see nothing. Then I saw feet. In horror, I looked up into Wulf's eyes. He was sitting in one corner of the room, in the shadows watching me like a hawk.

I leaped away from the sacks as if they had bitten me and sat down heavily on my bed.

'How long . . . when . . . did you come in here?' My voice was tight with alarm.

Wulf smiled superciliously, but said nothing. I was desperate, embarrassed, on the defensive. Instinctively, I struck out.

'My priests tell me that the sorcerers of your land use trickery to gain the allegiance of the peasants. That your stories of elves are fabrications. And if not that, then they are evil, for it means you are consorting with devils.'

There was a silence. I sat stiffly, holding my breath, waiting for an explosion of anger from Wulf. But there was none. To my astonishment he chuckled.

'It is true that some sorcerers try to impress with trickery. But the people usually see through that. Recently there was a sorcerer in this area who could swallow a burning brand and sharp pieces of flint. But for all this, he was still not considered to be a powerful sorcerer for he could not always summon the spirits.'

Wulf stood up, walked over to his bed and rearranged the sacks as they had been before I had interfered with them.

'If you are so interested in the plants I use, you can come with me into the forest tomorrow, in search of more power-plants. Meeting you at the beach and bringing you here has delayed my hunting.'

I looked at him in surprise. Not once had it occurred to me that I had been doing anything other than accompanying him on his usual business. And when I thought of the reception he had received at the settlement – the gifts, the guest-house and the arrangements for the healing sessions – it seemed inconceivable that his arrival had not been anticipated.

'But Wulf, surely they expected you at the settlement, or the horse might have died. They must have sent for you?'

He shook his head firmly. 'They never know when to expect me. Of course I went to the settlement to heal the horse, but it was sick because it was important that you saw it healed, just as the two warriors fought because it was vital for you to understand how we deal with death.'

I stared at him blankly.

'Everything that has happened took place because you arrived. If you had not come here, the warrior might still be alive and the horse might not have been sick. A man has been killed, and a horse healed, for your benefit.'

For a moment I was shocked but then, suddenly, I understood. Although the battle between the thanes must have been fortuitous, the horse-healing had been carefully prearranged to convince me of Wulf's powers. I thanked God for forcing the truth from the mouth of the charlatan, although since I had been taken in completely by the deception I could not understand why Wulf should now be freely admitting to it. Eappa's warning sounded in my ears: 'Beware of the heathen, for they have the cunning of the devil.'

'The horse was made to appear sick so that you could fake a cure,' I stated coldly. 'The cure was a fraud.'

Wulf chuckled. 'Of course. We had a serious discussion with the horse and explained to him that he must pretend to be sick.'

Wulf's sarcasm left me unconvinced, for the animal's sickness could have been induced by some herbal means before my arrival.

'The horse was really sick,' Wulf insisted. 'But if we had not come to the settlement, perhaps it would not have been sick.'

'Are you saying that our going to the settlement made it sick?'

'I did not say that. We no more made the horse sick than its being sick made us go to the settlement. It is not a question of one thing causing the other. Rather, they arise together, held up by the web of wyrd. Your Mission, the dead warrior, the sick horse and my presence were bound together as surely as sun, showers and a rainbow. Sorcery killed the warrior and made the horse sick, just as sorcery delivered you to our shores to witness these events.'

'You mean, charms were cast, binding spells made?' My words clacked from a dry mouth. Being tricked was abominable, but the thought of being an unwitting victim of sorcery was more than I could stomach.

Wulf looked at me non-committally, his expression calm and relaxed.

'Not necessarily,' he said. 'By sorcery, I mean the forces that rule Middle-Earth. I have told you that, for the sorcerer, everything vibrates the web or wyrd, whether it is an act of the gods or the movement of the tiniest insect. Your arrival trembled the web. The flight of the ravens trembled the web. My presence vibrates the web. The battle of warriors and the sick horse trembled the web. All our lives are locked together in the shimmering world of wyrd in which all things are enmeshed, and connected to one another by the threads of wyrd.'

I had been impressed by Wulf's explanation of a web which contained all things, but now that I was supposedly caught within it, the idea seemed sinister and I could not accept it.

Wulf reached over and fingered the sleeve of my tunic. 'The weave of this cloth reveals to us the pattern of wyrd,' he said. 'Your individual destiny is laid out on a loom. All the incidents in your life, all the dreams, thoughts, fears, are a pattern woven on to the loom. The duration of your life is measured by the vertical thread, held taut by the weights of life-force. The horizontal threads of the loom are the forces to be encountered during the course of your life, rather than days and nights. The pattern woven on to this loom is the pattern of your life, and the pattern is woven by the Three Sisters of Wyrd.'

I breathed a deep sigh of relief for I knew now that Wulf had not attempted to delude me and that his healing exploits were genuine. His error was simply in believing that disparate events were joined in some way other than being part of God's Kingdom. Only by the hand of the Lord could events be connected without regard to time or location. And in the Three Sisters of Wyrd I knew now the basis for his bizarre beliefs; in Mercia I had heard that warriors told tales of female spirits, three wild women who were dealers in death, choosing in battle those who would die and those who would live. But in truth the teachings of Christ the Saviour would not allow us to believe such superstition, for it rested on the blasphemous belief that our lives were under the control of such spirits. My memory fed me Eappa's words: 'When the Creator made mankind, he gave free will to the first people.' Confidently, I retaliated.

'Wulf, I cannot allow myself to believe that life is controlled by such forces, for our God teaches that individuals are born of free will. Even when people transgress God's command and obey the devil, they become guilty through their own free will.'

Wulf looked at me, his brow furrowed in obvious puzzlement. 'The devil? Is this a spirit?'

I felt a spasm of unease. 'He is not to be dwelt on, Wulf. Know only that he is anathema to our God.'

'But how are people influenced by this "devil", if he is not a spirit with powers?'

'By free will. People go against the laws of God by free will and are therefore drawn by the accursed devil.'

Wulf did not seem able to grasp my argument. The blessed truth of God's gift of free will was beyond him. He lay back on the bed and gazed into the roof-thatch. Eventually he rolled over to face me again.

'There is no need for your free will. Although the Wyrd Sisters spin the web of wyrd and weave the loom of life, they do not thereby determine it, for they are agents of wyrd and are therefore just as much a part of the pattern of wyrd as we. The Wyrd Sisters simply express the will of wyrd. And so do we. We cannot control our lives, because we too are inseparable aspects of wyrd and express its will. But this is not the same as saying our life is determined. Rather, it is saying we live like an ocean voyager, trimming our sails to the winds and tides of wyrd as we skim across the waters of life. And cresting the waves of wyrd is something that happens at every instant. The pattern of life is not woven ahead of time, like cloth to be worn later as a tunic. Rather, life is woven at the very instant you live it.'

I stared at the weave of my tunic. Wulf seemed to be talking in riddles, but I was intrigued by his convictions.

'Wulf, how does a person who shares your views live in accord with wyrd? If there is no free will, how can someone change his life for the better?'

'Patterns change as they are woven. A pattern that is complex has more scope for change, for there are many themes on which a new pattern may be based. But even the simplest of lives changes over the course of time. The task of a sorcerer is to become fully aware and sensitive to all nuances of his life-design as it unfolds.

Aware, as the weaver, of all the forces that impinge upon the pattern – all colours, shapes, textures. With a weaver like wyrd, there are no limits to the possible designs and we can never fully appreciate all of our own design. But we can try.'

I thought about my life and the important decisions I had taken and those that had been made for me. I could understand the essence of Wulf's view, but could not accept it.

'You do not have to worry about it,' Wulf chuckled, reading the uncertainty on my face. 'The important thing is that you are bound to encounter the spirits and the Wyrd Sisters, as surely as you are bound one day to die.'

He lay back on his mattress and closed his eyes while I regarded him with a strange mixture of condescension and awe. His healing powers would be miraculous were it not that they stemmed from devils rather than the Almighty. Yet I could not dismiss his healing of the horse from my mind, and his alien and esoteric views of life – even the way he spoke and moved – seemed to flow from some inner resource inaccessible to me. Although I hardly dared admit the thought into my mind, I realised there were strong parallels between Wulf and Eappa, for both possessed an ineffable sense of inner strength and direction. Then, in compensation for my temerity in comparing a servant of God with a pagan, I immediately dwelt on their differences: Wulf was more outgoing and effusive, whereas Eappa carefully controlled those parts of his inner self that he allowed the world to see. Wulf was certainly much more unpredictable; disturbingly so. But his sometimes startling changes of mood and action might have had more to do with my inability to understand the bases for his actions than with any instability in himself.

Suddenly Wulf swung his feet to the floor and leaned towards me, as if he had made a decision. The speed of his movement startled me and I spun around to face him. He peered at me probingly, waiting for me to settle.

'All that you heard about the elves was just so much ox-dung,' he said softly. 'What I told those people was not a lie. But words are such feeble shadows in describing the world of the spirits that they might as well have been lies. The eyes of an ordinary person are capable of seeing only the most obvious signs of wyrd, as if a clear sky contained the moon but no shining stars. There are many, many more forces which, unseen by us, impinge on our lives at every step. These forces are the spirits, which are subtle emanations of wyrd. The peasants know they are there and see the effects they have, but cannot see or deal with them directly. The eyes of a child can sometimes glimpse the world of spirits, but the adult is too wary to allow such visions to penetrate his armour. As a sorcerer I mediate between the people and the world of the spirits. It is this task for which the people value my services.'

For a moment I was overwhelmed by his sudden intensity. His eyes shone with the disturbing gleam I had seen in the paddock earlier in the day. He obviously wanted to talk but I looked away from him, unsure how to respond.

'Do you truly believe that you can communicate with the spirits?' I said at last.

He sat back and spread his arms wide, as if the answer were self-evident. 'I see them. I hear them. I talk to them.'

'Do you *control* them, Wulf?'

He shook his head once, firmly. 'I love, hate, cajole and fight the spirits, but there can be no question of my controlling them. The balance of power between the sorcerer and the spirits is precarious; it must be maintained with great care and tact. In return, the spirits enable the sorcerer to traverse the webs that lead into all worlds: of the gods, Middle-Earth and the dead.'

As I watched him talk, his entire body seemed to tremble like a butterfly newly hatched. His whole demeanour was strangely unsettling.

He leaned forward again eagerly.

'The spirits are ready for you, Brand, they are seeking you out. In the stable compound, when I went to get my staff to drive the forces of sickness from the horse, I saw a spirit standing right behind you. I had to pull it away from you with my eyes.'

I stared at him, thunderstruck.

'He was right by your shoulder, and looking directly at you,' Wulf went on.

I knew that I was listening to the histrionics of a heathen. Missionaries before me had confirmed the reality of such devils, but Wulf's claim that I would encounter spirits at his bidding, before his eyes, was absurd. Yet my fears were growing rapidly.

'Was I in danger?' I asked meekly, cringing with embarrassment as I heard my cowardly question.

'Possibly. We do not yet know how the spirits will deal with you. If you become aware of the spirits near you, it is imperative that you hold your rune-stick out in your hand, like this.' He held out his hand with the forefinger extended, as if along the length of the rune-stick; his other fingers curled under to grip the imaginary stick at its base.

I was aware that my fear was increasing by leaps and bounds, despite the fact that only moments before I had dismissed all concerns about the spirits from my mind.

'But Wulf, why should the spirits wish to hurt me? I have done them no harm.'

He laughed derisively, startling me again and I bit my lip in an attempt to control my panic.

'The spirits are afraid of you,' he rasped. 'You come here with a new god, belittle the spirits as devils and plot to replace me with shaven monks. The spirits will treat you warily; they will want to take you away, on their terms, in order to discover your true intentions. They will not give up their secrets unless they believe you are sincere in your quest, for if you are not then you will use your new-found knowledge against them.'

'But Wulf, you said your spirits would show me the true depths of your beliefs. Now you tell me that they *might* reveal their secrets but that they are just as likely to be hostile towards me. What am I to believe?'

'No one knows how the spirits will deal with them,' he said gently. 'Even our own people are sometimes rejected by them. Any attempt to enter the world of spirits is a risk. Death is always a possibility. But we shall go into the forest tomorrow and the spirits will come to you. One thing is certain: they sought you out in the paddock and they will seek you out in the forest. They are moving towards you along the threads of your web; all we can do is to try to ensure that you are as well prepared as possible. For if you fail to heed their messages, the spirits will capture your soul without your knowledge and, like a plant robbed of its root, you will wither and die.'

PART TWO

Journeys into the Spirit World

8

THE WYRD SISTERS

IN THE silver light of dawn, we slipped out of the house and walked through the centre of the settlement along the path leading north to the great forest. Roof thatches dripped with night rainfall and rivulets of water still ran from sloping roofs and tinkled into deep-dug drainage ditches. Two lean watchdogs splashed after us, sniffing at our scent in the early morning breeze, then lost interest and dropped away. Soon we were clear of the houses and skirting open farmland, crop fields stretching away to the west, divided into strips by grassy baulks and bounded by headland bumpy from turning ploughs.

The sweet smell of wet, ploughed earth brought a sudden rush of memories. My random thoughts, still wrapped in the thrall of slumber, gradually gave way to images of my father working the patchwork of fields surrounding the monastery. He farmed strips of common land also, but his summers were spent working the monastic fields with the help of my older brothers. When I reached seven winters I had joined them in the fields, proudly carrying out my hoe at dawn and trudging back tired and hungry at dusk. But I had been even prouder when, some years later, the monks had selected me for instruction in writing, reading and – latterly – scripture. I loved especially the work in the scriptorium and, as I walked, the images of fields were replaced by the smell of ink and the feel of crackle-dry parchment.

Eventually the shrill music of early morning birdsong faded and the low mist slipped away to reveal a pink sky. Wulf threaded a path through thinly wooded glades bordering the forest and after a time began to track the course of a stream. Our progress was slowed by pools of enormous bankside ferns and huge shrubs of creamy-flowered elder forced us to make long detours.

We walked all day, stopping to rest only twice; the first time was at noon, to drink from a clear stream, then again later to sit in a shady spot and cool our feet in a still pool.

By late afternoon we were deep into the forest. Wulf led the way on to a river bank and pointed into the trees. At the top of a sloping, grassy bank, twenty feet from the water and hidden against a backdrop of alder and beech, nestled a small man-made shelter. I was astonished, for we were miles from the pig-droving road which cut into the forest from Cydda's farm and I had been told that no other roads or trails traversed this part of the kingdom. Wulf explained that he had constructed the camp because this was a place of power and from here I would encounter the spirits.

The shelter was well built: a sloping roof, covered with turf, leaned against a heavy branch fixed horizontally between two conveniently placed birch trees. The entrance, facing towards the river, was screened by two wattle hurdles lashed to the structure by rope and chinked in with moss, reeds and leafy twigs. One of the hurdles was attached to an upright stake with rope hinges and served as a door.

I helped Wulf to set up the camp, clearing debris from the fire-pit and flinging armfuls of fallen leaves and twigs into the undergrowth. Then Wulf constructed a fishing pole from a long bough cut from a low-hanging willow and twine from one of his sacks, while I dug for bait in the soft earth above the river bank.

Before long I was fishing from a large, flat rock just above the waterline, while Wulf waded up river in search of watercress and vegetables. Lazily, I threw the bait into the river and leaned back to wait for a bite. I felt relieved that the day had so far passed without incident, but I knew that I could not count on peace and quiet for long. Wulf was a man of consummate confidence and assurance and he was adamant that I would encounter the spirits. I also knew that, having come across this far with Wulf, I was committed to working with him on his terms. Whatever happened from this point on was surely in the hands of the Lord.

I closed my eyes, slipped my hand inside the tunic, clasped my crucifix and murmured the Lord's Prayer.

Eventually I lifted my heavy eyelids to see lengthening afternoon shadows sneaking out across the river and clouds of darting gnats emerging from the shelter of the trees. Brown-winged alder-flies struggled just above the water, buffeted by the gentle breeze as though it were a raging storm. I watched the current gurgling past my feet, swirling broad and deep around a wide bend and disappearing under a dense overhang of black-barked alder. Across the water the opposite bank crowded with beech and willow, roots clawing the waterline like giant, curling toes, partly covered with clumps of spiky, purple balls of watermint and forget-me-nots. It was a beautiful and tranquil setting. Drowsily, my eyes sank slowly shut.

Suddenly I snapped fully alert, my body tensed, though I had no idea what alarmed me. The river bank lay deserted and eerily silent; all birdsong had ceased. Then I heard, just barely, a low rumbling sound which seemed to float on the breeze from across the river. I stared wide-eyed into the undergrowth, but could see nothing unusual. Vaguely, I became aware of the fishing pole slipping from my grasp into the water.

Glimpsing movement up river, I dug my bare toes into the rock ready for running, but then I saw that it was Wulf paddling slowly under the willow and alder overhang, his hands piled high with bunches of watercress. I swallowed hard, trying to regain some sense of composure.

Wulf splashed on to the bank and stood for a moment, examining me closely. Then he began to laugh.

'Where is the fishing pole?' he asked, raising his eyebrows in mock curiosity.

With a sinking heart I remembered that I had dropped it. 'In the water,' I said sheepishly.

'You should not have been surprised,' he said softly, suddenly serious. 'The spirits have been following us all day. Did you not hear them earlier?'

I gaped at him. I knew that there was no way he could have heard the buzzing sound from his position down river.

'Hurry up!' Wulf said. 'We have to collect firewood before dusk falls.'

In a daze, I paddled into the river to retrieve the pole and, collecting the one trout I had caught, hurried up the bank to join Wulf at the fire-pit. Under the shade of the trees, he had dug a food store; now we dropped the watercress and the fish into the hole in the ground, carefully covered them over and scattered leaves to camouflage the area.

Then Wulf led the way down river and along a deer trail that cut deeper into the forest, collecting and stacking loose firewood on the way for us to pick up on our return to the camp. Eventually we emerged from a coppice of hazel into a long, broad meadow. Setting sunlight slanted through the surrounding tree cover like golden javelins and around the perimeter of the meadow, birch, beech and occasional oaks floated in a sea of green and yellow fern.

Suddenly I saw Wulf standing rigidly upright, nostrils flared, sniffing as if for the scent of the wild boar. Nervously I scanned the surrounding trees and shrubs, but saw nothing of consequence. Then I heard, or rather felt, a faint vibration under my feet and stood rooted to the spot as the sensation grew into an ominous rumble. Wulf's head jerked around and he pointed straight-armed towards the far end of the glade, directly under the shade trees. The ground shimmered with a thick covering of pale blue clover which was undulating like an incoming tide. As I stared at the spot, I realised that the movement was caused by a swarm of bees bustling in and out of the clover, droning just above ground level.

'The Lord be blessed!' I blurted out in relief. 'It was only bees all the . . .' Wulf silenced me with a frantic wave of his arm.

'Those bees are the Wyrd Sisters,' he hissed. 'Come on!'

Wulf started running towards the tree cover, his body bent double; I scrambled after him, hurling myself into the ferns at the edge of the glade. Wulf swept off his hat and knelt low, watching the bees through waving fern fronds. Craning my neck over his shoulder, I stared unblinking down the glade. The bees were at least fifty paces distant, too far away to see in detail.

'The Wyrd Sisters have come to loosen your fibres,' he breathed, his eyes still fixed on the bees. 'That will make it possible for you to encounter the spirits by travelling along your personal web of power. Brand, you must go to meet them. Show them you are available and that you want to be helped.'

I half stood, determined to leave. 'Wulf, I don't want to. I cannot do it. Let us get out of the forest.'

But he gripped my arm in a grasp like an iron clamp.

'We cannot do that, Brand. It is not possible. If you try to run they will know that you are not sincere in your wish to learn our secrets and they will kill you.'

He opened his mouth to speak again, but then turned away to glance down the meadow once more, keeping his grip on my arm.

'Now listen carefully,' he commanded, spitting out the words in a hissing whisper. 'Walk slowly and softly towards them. When you get close, within ten paces, turn your back on them and walk away. If they ignore you, then they are not ready for you! Do you understand?'

I nodded stiffly, my heart pounding.

'But Wulf, what happens if they are ready for me?'

'Then the Wyrd Sisters will loosen your fibres.'

'How?'

Wulf ignored the question. He was again peering over the ferns towards the bees and I did not move.

'Go!' Wulf said, pushing me out of the undergrowth. I stepped into the clearing and stood rigidly, staring down the meadow. I had become accustomed to following Wulf's instructions and, indeed, had accepted this as a necessary part of the arrangements by which I might enter and understand his pagan world. But as I stared at the seething swarm I shivered uncontrollably. I did not know whether I was approaching bees or spirits but, if Wulf did indeed discourse with devils, I could be facing death. I glanced heavenward, but the Lord's Prayer stuck in my throat. I was approaching devils of my own free will and I had no right to ask for His help. I took a deep breath and began to steal slowly down the glade towards the bees. Twice I faltered and had to force myself to take further steps. Finally I stopped ten paces from the droning swarm, where I waited, holding my breath. Sweat ran freely from my temples and dripped from my chin. I stood for what seemed an age while the swarm rumbled monotonously, the low drone almost soporific. Gradually I began to relax; they sounded like a normal swarm of contentedly foraging bees and I could see nothing unusual in their behaviour. They did not appear to be at all interested in me. Either the spirits were not ready for me or, much more likely, Wulf had been mistaken and the bees were nothing more than they appeared. With a sigh of relief I turned on my heel and strode back up the glade. Immediately the droning grew louder and I darted a glance over my shoulder just in time to see the bees forming a dense cloud a foot above the clover. Simultaneously I felt a strong grip on my left shoulder and found that Wulf was standing beside me.

'Walk backwards. Slowly,' he ordered, his voice harsh and commanding, cutting across the noise of the swarm. 'Do not turn your back on them, Brand. Those bees have the power of the Sisters; they have come to loosen your fibres.'

We began to move backwards, Wulf seeming to glide noiselessly over the clover. I slowed my movements to match his and we moved away from the bees almost imperceptibly. But the bees swarmed higher, the drone rising in pitch until it filled the glade with a piercing whine. I was struggling with an almost irresistible urge to turn and run when Wulf signalled for me to halt.

'Take off your right shoe,' he ordered, gesturing urgently towards my feet. I stared at him in panic, thinking that I had not heard him correctly. Wulf's eyes narrowed to slits, his face taut with concentration.

'Hurry! Do as I say.'

Immediately I dropped to one knee and began to unwrap my shoe. My hands trembled and the leather knots resisted my frantic fingers. With the straps half untied, I tore the shoe from my foot and flung it aside.

Wulf whipped off the thongs around his right leg, took off his own shoe and began pulling hard at the clover near his feet.

'Clear a patch of earth and put your bare foot on to it. Fast!'

He was now having to shout in order to be heard over the whine.

Desperately I scrabbled at the clover, repeatedly glancing at Wulf and then down the glade towards the bees. He continued digging his fingers into the soil and piling earth next to him, then he slammed his bare foot on to the exposed patch of ground. I placed my own foot on the bare earth I had cleared.

The bees swarmed above head height and Wulf turned to me. 'They are coming after you, Brand. Get ready.'

I did not know what I was supposed to do. I was rooted to the spot, kneeling on the ground with my bare foot on the earth and quite unable to take any positive action. I began to murmur the Lord's Prayer, forcing it through clenched teeth, swallowing hard after every line. Then the bees came, moving slowly like a gigantic, deadly cloud. Crouching, Wulf snatched up a handful of soil, leaped prodigiously into the air and in the same movement hurled the soil into the swarm. His voice was a hoarse shriek:

> *Settle, Wyrd Women,*
> *Swoop to the ground.*
> *Unfetter the bonds*
> *that lie around Brand.*

The bees hurtled towards me like a quiver of screaming arrows. Panic-stricken, I whirled around and plunged headlong up the meadow, slipping and slithering on grass suddenly wet with pouring rain, running so fast that I could hardly stretch my legs far enough to keep up with my body. Rain arrows bit into the ground all around me and then something hit me hard from behind. I recoiled from the blow, spun around and the ground slammed into me. Rolling over and over, tasting blood, with the roar of the bees all around me, I landed on my back and saw the sky blackened by an enormous rain cloud. As I watched in horror, the cloud twisted and swirled into the shapes of three immense women, spitting flames across the sky. These monster women swooped screaming out of the sky, spectres crowding through the air and heading straight towards me, crackling sheets of arrows pouring from their bellies and flashing into my body. The wind tore a scream from my lips and in desperation I snatched the rune-stick from my neck, grasped it tightly in my right hand and flung it at the women with all of my strength. With a great crack of light, the monsters swept away from me into the swirling sky, churning like some storming ocean. I looked around wildly for the bees, but they had gone. I sank back into the sopping grass, dizzy and sick; then darkness descended and blotted everything out.

When I recovered consciousness it was still dark. I tried to heave myself into a sitting position, but a blinding bolt of pain flashed behind my eyes and scorched down my neck. I lay still, breathing hard, allowing the nightmare to slip away into the soft embrace of darkness. Sweat lay wet on my face and neck. My body felt on fire and a dull pain throbbed down my left side. After a time I realised that my clothes were missing and I was wrapped up in a blanket.

Suddenly a painfully bright light pierced the darkness. I shut my eyes tightly and then felt something cool cover my forehead. Forcing my eyes open, I looked up into Wulf's smiling face. I tried to smile back, but a stabbing pain in my side twisted my expression into a grimace.

'The Wyrd Sisters have loosened your fibres,' he said, beaming. 'Your fibres can now move freely according to the tides and currents of wyrd, the positions of the stars, the pattern of the sun and moon and the most insignificant of distant events. With your fibres able to move freely, your soul can travel through your shield-skin to the land of the spirits.'

Although I could hear his words, his voice sounded tiny and muffled like the faint scratchings of field-mice in a grain store.

Wulf removed his palm from my forehead and, in silence, peeled back the blanket. Gritting my teeth, I raised my hand and peered into the light to see what was causing the pain in my side. My body was covered with a mass of small red swellings concentrated especially across the stomach where they merged into one streak of red like an open wound.

Wulf gently pushed my head back and then eased me over on to my stomach. I could feel him passing his hands lightly over my back.

'Your shield-skin had dried to a crust, like the shell of a tortoise,' he said. 'It was rigid and unyielding. It is a wonder that the fibres of wyrd could tremble into your body at all. But the Wyrd Sisters have cracked your shield-skin and the first barrier to the spirit world has been broken.'

Periodically Wulf stopped, grunted and explored a particular area of my body, prodding firmly with what felt like the heel of his palm. When he pushed into my back I felt a strangely pleasant tingling sensation deep inside my body.

Wulf rolled me over again on to my back and began to run his hands across my chest and stomach. I yelped with pain when he pressed into my left side and I tried to speak, but my mouth was dry and I only mumbled.

'A strong thread enters your body here,' he explained. 'It is a vital fibre, trapped until now by your rigid shield-skin. Now that it can move, you will have access to great powers.'

When he had finished he sat up, clucking like a disapproving parent. 'With your fibres so rigid, the spirits would have ripped apart your threads like the flimsy web of a money spider.'

I gazed up at him, dazed, my mind empty of thoughts. He smiled again, perhaps in encouragement.

'Now, lie still and let me seal your fibres.'

He pushed the door wide open and stepped out; it was only then that I realised that I was lying in his shelter deep in the forest. Cautiously I raised myself up on one elbow and looked through the open doorway. Across the river, above the trees, the sky was stained lilac by the setting sun; it was possible that I had slept through an entire night and a day. I squinted towards the fire-pit; a fire blazed, sending splinters of blinding firelight into my eyes and I had to look away quickly and blink back the tears. When I turned back I could see the black silhouette of Wulf crouching by the fire-pit, holding a long wooden stake which was stripped clean of twigs and leaves. I watched him with a kind of detached interest as he thrust one end of the stake into the fire, then pulled it out sizzling and steaming and knocked the burning end on the side of a cooking pot set on the stone hob at the back of the fire-pit. Flakes of burning bark showered from the stick and hissed into the bowl.

Wulf returned the smoking stick to the flames and repeated the procedure twice; then he stood up, hooked the stake through the handle of the pot, pulled the pot from the hob and carried it into the shelter. He set the pot on the ground and I leaned forward to see over the rim; the pot was about half-full with a frothy green and white paste.

He squatted on the other side of the pot, took the stake and again stirred the mixture, sniffing and testing its consistency by lifting the stirring stick from the bowl and watching the liquid run slowly back into the pot. My nostrils filled with a powerful aroma faintly reminiscent of sweet ale.

Wulf opened his fist to reveal a small cake of soap, dried and cracked with age. 'Cup your hands,' he said, demonstrating what he wanted me to do by interlacing the fingers of his own hands. With his knife he shredded small slivers of the soap into my upturned fingers; then putting the remainder of the soap bar carefully to one side, he picked up the cooking pot.

'Hold your hands open and still,' he instructed. He tipped the pot over my hands and the thick liquid crawled slowly from the base of the pot, oozed down the side and dripped on to my fingers, still warm. He counted the drops, then tipped the pot back to an upright position and set it down.

'Now mix it together,' he said, again demonstrating with his hands. I ground my palms together in a circular motion, using my interlaced fingers as a pivot, and could feel the soap softening as I mixed it with the oily residue of the paste.

After a brief interval, Wulf tipped another nine drops of the liquid into my cupped fingers. I continued kneading and this time the mixture immediately became soft and sticky. Wulf reached out and gently pulled my hands apart and I saw that my palms and fingers were covered with a greenish-grey frothy lather. Grasping my left wrist, Wulf guided my hands up to my forehead and then held my hair back with one hand while with the other he wiped my fingers over my forehead. He did the same with my other hand and kept rubbing until my forehead was covered with the substance. It dried very quickly, and formed a crust; as it dried, it seemed to shrink and it felt as if a thick band around my head was being steadily tightened.

'It feels strange,' I said after a while. My tongue felt thick and clumsy. 'Why did you wipe this stuff all over me?'

I tried to stand up, but my head felt as light as a bubble, as if I were floating up to twice my normal height. I sat down heavily.

'Why did you wipe this on me?' I repeated indistinctly. I was alarmed by the fact that I seemed to be losing control of my tongue and my head was beginning to feel hot.

'This will seal your shield-skin,' he said reassuringly.

Wulf pulled the blanket from my body and gently pushed me down on to my back. Working rapidly, he poured the sticky substance all over me, then sliced more tiny segments of soap over me as if seasoning a dish of food. Finally he took several large plant leaves and rubbed the mixture over my body, mixing the soap and strange substance into a thick paste. With the leaves he smeared the mixture over my arms and legs, though I noticed that he took care not to touch the paste with his own hands. As he worked, he began to sing softly:

> *I have bound over the wounds*
> *with the best of healing amulets,*
> *That the wounds may neither burn nor burst,*
> *Nor putrify or grow worse,*
> *May they go no further, nor spread,*
> *May they not increase, nor the sores deepen,*
> *For this man has had fibres re-set,*
> *And the spirits will visit him.*

When he had finished he sat back on his heels.

'Your fibres have been freed and your soul may now journey out of your body and into the spirit-world. But you are not yet ready to encounter the spirits in their own land: that is why I have protected you. The layer of paste is formed from powerful plants and it will prevent your soul from slipping out of your body and travelling unchecked. But the paste will not last long and cannot be renewed. Before it loses its strength we must increase your life-force. Tomorrow we shall begin to hunt for power.'

Wulf picked up the pot, carried it outside and returned it to the fire-pit. I sat up slowly, my head spinning as I looked down at my body. The substance had dried to a thin, dark crust all over my skin. I rubbed my fingers on the crust, but it was set hard and I had a sudden, absurd attack of panic; my thoughts floundered about and settled on the certainty that I would never be able to remove the crust from my skin. Glancing up to ensure that Wulf was not yet returning to the shelter, I spat several times into my palm and rubbed furiously on the right side of my stomach. The greenish crust dissolved slowly to reveal a pink patch of skin still covered with tiny red bumps. Satisfied, I looked around again to locate Wulf but he had disappeared. I resumed my examination of the patch of skin, totally absorbed — my mind empty, head still feeling light as a puff of wind. With my forefinger, I very carefully touched one of the red bumps and immediately a tremendous thrill – half pleasure half pain – shot through my body and climbed up my back. For an instant I reeled with dizziness, and then my sense of balance returned. I gazed in wonder at the patch of skin, glowing red against the surrounding darkness of the crusty paste. I was both impressed and frightened. I knew now that my fibres had been truly loosened and that in truth the bees had been the Wyrd Sisters.

9

THE SPIRITS STEAL MY SOUL

THE AROMA of cooking food drifted into the shelter on the evening breeze and I struggled outside to see Wulf squatting near the fire-pit, a small mound of washed vegetables laid out on dock leaves at his side. I shuffled to the fire-pit, sat heavily on the log and picked absently through the food: young dandelion leaves, tiny onions, spinach, two small parsnips and a few mushrooms. Wulf headed, tailed and cleaned a black and silver trout, then wrapped it in large leaves and set it to bake in the embers of the fire on a cradle of smooth river-stones.

I watched the flames licking around the stones, drying the curling leaf-wrapping to a crisp brown. My mind still felt blank. In the shelter, I tried to recall the details of the incident with the Wyrd Sisters but all I could remember was the terror. I leaned closer to the fire and stared like a simpleton into the smoke spiralling above the blaze. Wulf turned the leaf-wrapped fish with a long stick, then tossed on to the fire a handful of herbs to dispel drifting clouds of gnats venturing from the river under cover of approaching dusk.

'Wulf, why did the Wyrd Sisters loosen my fibres?'

He shrugged his shoulders. 'I have told you. Once we have increased your life-force, your soul will be able to travel along your trembling fibres of wyrd into the world of the spirits.'

Wulf jabbed his charred stick into the sizzling leaf-pack and the aroma of cooking fish filled my nostrils. It made me feel slightly sick. He pulled the fish from the fire, peeled off the heat-dried leaves with his knife and sliced up the white meat. Then he ladled vegetables on to a platter, speared chunks of fish with his stick and handed it to me. Normally my mouth ran wet at the sight of fresh-cooked fish, but now I was not hungry. My stomach felt uncomfortably full.

Wulf looked at me and smiled broadly. 'No food? That is a very encouraging sign. It often happens that a person preparing to meet spirits loses interest in food.'

He took a mouthful of fish and chewed thoughtfully. 'Mmmm, Brand, this is delicious,' he chuckled, smacking his lips noisily. Then he got up and dipped a cup into the pot he had placed at the back of the hob and passed it to me.

'Lemon balm tea,' he said encouragingly.

I sipped cautiously at the steaming pale green liquid and found it refreshing, but small cramps of fear ran through my stomach.

'Wulf, I don't want to encounter any more spirits. The Wyrd Sisters were terrifying. I cannot go through that again; I want to return to the settlement.'

I was almost as surprised as Wulf to hear my statement. I had not deliberated about leaving the forest, but as soon as I had blurted out my fears I knew them to be true. I was ashamed to admit defeat so early, but I felt sure that another encounter with the Wyrd Sisters would surely kill me.

Wulf stopped eating, slowly put down his food and turned towards me. He scrutinised me in silence for a moment.

'Preparing to meet the spirits always induces fear, even terror,' he said softly. 'There is great uncertainty and danger, especially since you are alien to the spirit world of this kingdom. But the spirits have beautiful aspects too. And if they reveal to you the ways of wyrd, you will have that truth with you always, even as you return to the follies of Middle-Earth. You seek the nature of our gods to serve another, but I tell you that the mysteries of wyrd will bring joys and triumphs beyond comprehension. Your efforts will be worthwhile.'

I looked at him through misty eyes and I felt tears trickling down my cheeks. Suddenly, surprisingly, Wulf reached out and wiped the tears away with the back of his hand.

'Brand, you are a man of the spirits, though you do not know it yet. You are wolf-bold to embark on this quest and I know that it is not easy. Trust me. You will not be sorry.'

I felt very small and vulnerable and rather shocked that my emotions had spilled over so easily. Normally I was in control of such forces, for Eappa had told me they were an indulgence.

Wulf again pushed the plate of food towards me and this time I took it, though I did not start eating. Instead, I tried to clear my mind of fears by concentrating on the sun as it dipped below the tree-line. Huge, jagged, black clouds spread like enormous ink stains across a crimson sky. On the opposite bank the trees melted into the descending darkness like hunched, prowling giants.

Suddenly Wulf snapped his head round and scanned the trees behind us. Warning pangs of fear crawled up my back and automatically I put a hand to my chest to feel the comforting bulk of the crucifix. Wulf turned back to face the fire and calmly continued eating. I looked at him questioningly, but he said nothing and did not even glance at me.

Nervously I picked at my food. The fish seemed to have no flavour and I chewed mechanically, jaws stiff with tension. Suddenly I shivered violently and dropped my food. My chest felt completely empty and, wheezing, I sucked in a long, rasping gasp of air. Wulf jumped up and slapped me on the back as if I were choking on food. Gradually I regained control of my breathing. When he was sure I was all right, he sat down and continued eating. I sat erect, watching and measuring each breath, trying to rid myself of a strange sensation in my stomach.

Suddenly Wulf stopped eating again. 'Do you hear that?' he murmured, his head cocked on one side, eyebrows raised quizzically as if he were discussing the location of a spring cuckoo.

I had heard nothing, but I nodded stiffly, guessing that he must have heard the buzzing sound again. The gloom of nightfall took a step closer to the fire. Desperately I cast around for a topic of conversation, anything to get Wulf talking again.

'Wulf, what happens to life-force when someone dies? Does it disappear?' My voice sounded small and distant.

Wulf nodded gently. 'If released properly, it will exist in snake form until it is time for it to be used again. But sometimes, because of evil magic, the life-force is trapped in the head at death and for ever flies around frantically trying to escape. That is why we see spectres at night as disembodied heads or, sometimes, as flying flames.'

It was reassuring to hear his voice, but I was still suffering from the peculiar empty sensation in my chest and I felt almost hollow. I placed my hands palms down on the ground in front of me and breathed deeply, trying to regain some sense of stability. My fingers felt numb.

'Brand, we must bury these with care and reverence.'

Wulf held out his hand and in the flickering firelight gleamed the skeleton of the fish we had eaten.

'Now?' I said, alarmed at the faintness of my voice. I coughed and spoke louder. 'It's too dark, surely? I can hardly see five paces from the fire.'

'In the river,' he insisted, standing up as if to accompany me. 'This fish lost its shield-skin when it stopped breathing. It lost its life-force because we have eaten and absorbed it. All it has remaining is its soul, retreated to the bones. We must return the skeleton, intact, to the water so that the soul may begin its journey to the Underworld, the Land of the Dead.'

I felt tired and weak and offered no further protest. Taking the bones in my cupped hands, I stepped carefully down to the river, feeling the way with my feet as my eyes peered blindly into the darkness. Wulf padded softly behind me.

I knelt at the water's edge and the river seemed to go silent. I could sense the pull of water running past the bank, but it offered almost no sound.

'You must thank the fish for feeding us,' Wulf instructed.

'Thank you for feeding us. My heart goes with you on your journey,' I said, loudly enough for Wulf to hear but believing none of it. I slipped the skeleton into the water and in an instant it was gone.

Suddenly I felt dizzy and limp. I had an overwhelming urge to drop into the water and be borne away with the skeleton, flowing and sailing down the river, peaceful and serene, taking no further part in life – no more struggles, doubts, fears. I wanted to drift for ever. Then a small warning voice cried out from deep within me and I fought my way back to my senses like climbing up from a deep dive – difficult and slow at first, then fast and easy, finally bursting out into the light. Slowly I stood up, legs trembling with the effort and backed away from the water. I turned and looked up the gentle rise towards the shelter. The fire burned brightly, like a seething mass of accursed souls, spitting and sparking through the night. I started to walk towards it, Wulf still ghosting along at my side, but saying nothing. As we neared the fire, I had a sudden, strong desire to urinate, as if I had drunk an entire bucket of ale. I made a detour towards our cesspit, dug in the ground behind bushes some thirty paces from the shelter. I saw Wulf return to the camp-fire.

As I weaved through the trees, lightheaded and dizzy, I tripped over a solid object and sprawled headlong into the grass. My misfortune struck me as hilarious. Chuckling merrily, I struggled to my feet and began to examine the ground for the cause of my fall, expecting to find a jutting tree root or rabbit hole. I could find nothing, however.

Wulf hurried through the trees and squatted at my side, putting an arm around me protectively.

'Where did you trip?' he whispered urgently.

Amused by his intense interest, I laughed and pointed to the spot where my foot had caught. He scrabbled around in the darkness, flattening the grass with his palms, but the search was fruitless. There were no objects which could have tripped me.

'It's all right, Wulf,' I said, very loudly. 'I will walk more carefully.'

I started to step towards the bushes in exaggerated slow motion, feeling forward with my toes to see whether I was about to trip, sniggering at my own antics.

'Shut up, you fool!' Wulf hissed.

I clamped my hand over my mouth, my shoulders still bobbing up and down with suppressed laughter.

'The spirits are here,' Wulf whispered hoarsely. 'They have been trying to suck out your soul. And when you went to release the fishbones, they made off with it.'

He seized me and hustled me back towards the fire. I stumbled along by his side, shocked into alertness by his statements and struggling to comprehend what he was saying.

'They took your soul from you,' he insisted, helping me to sit down on the log. 'For a few moments you were without a soul, an empty shell, but you tripped over the spirits as they tried to make off with it. There must be a guardian spirit watching over you, for that was a fortunate accident. If it had not happened, you might have died.'

I felt ice-cold now, all humour frozen out of me, the menace of spirits filling me with foreboding.

'But Wulf, you spread this paste all over my body to protect me. Why isn't it working? How did my soul escape?'

Wulf shook his head slowly. 'Normally the substance I prepared is sufficient to keep out any kind of force and I applied it very carefully. We must be dealing with very powerful spirits indeed.'

'But you said you could talk to the spirits. Well, talk to them – tell them who I am, tell them I am not ready yet.' My voice shook with emotion and I thought I was going to break down again. I fought to maintain control and some semblance of dignity. Fleetingly I thought of my family and my home and wondered whether I would ever see them again. Despite my efforts to disguise my fear, I felt my face puckering to cry.

'I'll abandon my Mission,' I said, my voice breaking into sobs. 'I am serious this time. Take me back to the settlement. I will return another time, another year.'

Wulf crouched in front of me and gripped my arm.

'It is too late for that,' he said firmly. 'There is no means by which we could get out of the forest safely, now that the spirits are after your soul. You are too vulnerable.'

'But what can we do then?' I whined, wringing my hands in anguish.

'I am going to look around, Brand. I want to be sure that the spirits have left us. I shall plant a web of power around this clearing; runes buried so that no forces may gain access to your soul while you are within their circle.'

Wulf jerked his head towards the shelter. 'Stay inside the shelter while I am gone and on no account open the door until I return. If you venture outside the shelter before I have planted the rune-sticks, you will be exposing yourself to great danger.'

He walked with me to the shelter, pulled open the wattle door and ushered me into the dark confines beneath the sloping roof. He crawled in with me, placed his hand on my shoulder briefly, then slipped out and shut the door behind him. I heard the rope latch slither into place and his footsteps padding into the distance. Then I lay alone in the shelter.

The little room was dark with shadows, though gradually my eyes sought out chinks of grey light which seeped in through the cracks, and light from the camp-fire flickered around the door frame. I sat in the blackness feeling numb and confused, but after a time I began to reflect on my behaviour. In particular, I was puzzled and a bit afraid of my wild swings in mood. Days ago, before embarking on this Mission, I had dedicated myself to the service of the Lord and prayed for His protection. Yet a short time ago I had been crying to be released from this forest. I felt ashamed; and a surprising quality entered my sense of shame: the awareness that I did not want Wulf to be disappointed in me. He seemed to be making a sincere attempt to lead me to his gods and I did not want to let him down.

Anger surged through my stomach; anger at myself for having been so weak and unworthy. And with the anger came renewed confidence, determination, will. I rolled over and crawled around the floor of the shelter searching for my bag. When I found it at the back of the shelter I fumbled blindly inside until I found three candles, fine quality altar candles which I had brought with me all the way from Mercia. Clearing away piles of moss, I pushed the bases of the candles into the earth floor. It took me a long time to trim the wicks in the dark, the knife feeling cumbersome in comparison with the small wick cutters we used in the monastery.

When the candles were ready, I pulled one from the ground, crawled to the door and lifted the latch cautiously. Wulf's warnings were in my mind, but I knew that I would have to light the candle from the camp-fire outside. The door creaked slightly ajar and I peered through the crack. Night had settled, but I could see the area immediately surrounding the fire-pit. Swinging the door open I ran to the fire, doubled over in some absurd attempt to remain unseen and lit the candle from the flames. Then I turned, cupping my hand around the candle-flame, and scuttled back into the shelter. The door clattered flimsily behind me and I stayed still for a moment on my hands and knees, gasping with relief, listening for sounds of spirits. There were none.

I lit the other candles and the room became lightly scented with the comforting aroma of beeswax. I placed two of the candles side by side, took the crucifix from around my neck and laid it on the ground between the candles. It seemed to glow in the soft light and spread a warmth around the room. I bent over and kissed the cross gently; then, grasping the third candle, I crawled to the rear of the shelter and stuck the base firmly in the ground; it drove away the menacing shadows that lurked under the angle where the sloping roof met the earth. As I straightened up, I felt a tickling sensation on my side and thinking that a spider had crawled inside my tunic, I slapped hard at the spot. Then I realised that it was a rune-stick. Delving deep inside my clothing, I pulled out the stick and examined it closely under the candle-light. It looked crude and clumsy, yet as I turned it towards the flickering flame the stick seemed to take on a warmth of its own. The carvings leaped into relief as light and shadow moved across the flat part of the stick, and the shapes seemed to me to be deeply familiar, as if I had carved them aeons ago. I rubbed my forefinger along the runes and felt a pleasurable tingling in my fingers. Carefully, I dropped the rune-stick back inside my tunic and tied shut the open neck of my clothing. In this land of spirits, even a pagan amulet offered some comfort.

* * *

Night thickened and still there was no sign of Wulf. My thoughts were forced to turn to more mundane matters: I had not relieved myself since early afternoon and now I needed desperately to urinate. At first I stalled, sitting in discomfort and waiting for Wulf to return. He had warned me not to leave the shelter and I had already risked one foray outside to light the candle from the fire. I considered – and dismissed – urinating in the shelter, for it would be utterly humiliating if Wulf were to find out. But as my need became even more urgent I resolved that I must go outside. I pressed my ear to the crack between the birch upright and the wattle door; I could hear nothing except the soft whisper of the night breeze and the familiar sound of night animals. Very slowly I pulled open the latch and peered out through the narrow slit. Black clouds crawled across the face of the moon and shadows crowded close to the fire. With a pounding heart I pulled open the door, stepped into the dim pool of firelight and, humming loudly, hurried quickly around the side of the shelter. I did not go as far as the cesspit but instead ventured only a few paces into the trees and stood there for several minutes. The forest was full of sounds and I could not urinate.

Suddenly there was a loud crack, something moved under my right foot and the bushes shuddered and trembled. Immediately I scrambled back into the shelter and slammed the door, almost pulling it from its hinges. I sat hugging myself, rocking back and forth in anguish, taking in deep, shuddering breaths to reassure myself that my soul had not been snatched again.

* * *

After an eternity the latch clicked and the door swung open. Wulf smiled at my startled expression.

'Did you think the spirits had got you?' he teased.

I tried to cover my embarrassment with humorous banter: I told Wulf that his idle warnings had cost me much discomfort, and explained that out of respect for his dire predictions I had debated for hours whether to go outside to relieve myself.

The door rattled shut behind him.

'You went outside?' he said, obviously shocked.

'No. That's why I am so pleased to see you,' I lied.

'You did the right thing,' Wulf said gravely.

He turned and opened the door quietly, stepping out in front of the shelter. I could see him framed against the night sky, swivelling his head slowly from right to left, surveying the area beyond the firelight and into the surrounding darkness.

Gesturing for me to follow him, Wulf walked away from the shelter towards the trees. Hurrying after him, I crossed the clearing and went to the place we used as a cesspit. I stood in the bushes and Wulf posted himself directly behind me, his back against mine, staring out into the surrounding darkness. The whole situation was absurd, but I was too apprehensive to protest.

When I had relieved myself, we walked back to the camp. Suddenly I felt a loud banging in my ears, as if a hammer were inside my head.

'Wulf, I can hear the buzzing again!' I yelled in panic. 'It's really loud.'

He grasped me by the arm and hustled me back towards the fire. In a hoarse whisper, he instructed me to sit with him, back-to-back, on the patch of ground between the shelter and the fire.

'We must let them come,' he hissed. 'You must see them. They cannot hurt you here, you are protected by a web of power. Runes are planted all around the clearing.'

I trembled violently. 'But Wulf, I'm terrified of the spirits: what will they do?'

'Sit still,' he grunted, settling his back firmly against mine. As long as you stay within this patch of ground, the spirits cannot now touch your soul.'

We sat for a long time. I hardly dared to breathe and my body crawled with sensations. My left foot became numb near the ankle, and then I developed a feeling of pressure and pain half-way down my back, on the right side. The muscles on my chest began to tighten. My buttocks became numb. The sensations grew in intensity until the back pain became unbearable, but I shifted position slightly and the pain disappeared.

'What's the matter?' Wulf whispered immediately.

I told him that my back had become stiff and painful, but moving it had cured the discomfort.

'You should have told me,' he said irritably. 'Do not take chances.'

Shortly afterwards I felt a burning sensation in both buttocks which worsened until I could hardly stand it.

'Wulf, my backside's burning,' I gasped.

'Push on your legs and lift your buttocks from the ground,' he ordered. Using Wulf's back as a brace, I tightened my leg muscles and eased my bottom a few inches from the ground. Almost immediately the pain went away.

'It's all right now,' I whispered and resumed my normal position.

We had been sitting for perhaps half the night when I had a sudden fit of yawning.

'What are you doing?' Wulf hissed.

'Yawning.'

'The spirits are here,' he snapped, suddenly leaping to his feet.

I fell flat on my back, arms flailing to regain balance and looking around wildly for some sign of the spirits; I could not protect myself from something I could not see. I rolled into a crouch and grabbed a heavy piece of firewood from the edge of the fire-pit, but Wulf took the club from my hand and tossed it to the ground.

'We do not need weapons for this,' he growled. 'The spirits are testing you. Show them your rune-stick and they will understand that you are not yet ready. But try to attack them and they will either kill you or disappear never to return. Then you will have come all this way for nothing.'

He helped me to my feet. 'Now follow me, and you may get a glimpse of them.'

Wulf crouched over and trotted out from under the tree cover on to the open river bank. I stayed close behind him. At the water's edge Wulf sank down on to his hands and knees and I did the same.

'Stay absolutely still,' he breathed. 'One careless movement and they will be on top of us.'

We lay motionless on the river bank, the surrounding trees barely lit by a pale moon. I could not see, hear or feel anything out of the ordinary, but I was tense with apprehension and excitement.

A cool breeze blew into my face and curved around the back of my raised head. It felt as if I were being pelted with feathers.

'Can you hear anything?' Wulf asked eventually, squinting at me through the darkness.

I was not sure what sort of sound I ought to be hearing.

'No,' I said. 'Only the breeze.'

He gripped my arm and stared at me wide-eyed. 'Did you feel a wind?' he demanded, his voice urgent and anxious.

I pointed ahead of us and to the right to indicate the source of the wind, near the down river end of the bank, just inside the tree cover.

Wulf stared in the direction of my pointing finger. Suddenly he tightened his grip on my arm. 'Can you see them?' he whispered excitedly. 'In the crack willow?'

I edged a little closer to him in order to look at the trees from the same vantage point, my eyes wide and staring, unblinking. It was difficult to make out anything about the tree except its huge bulk. In the darkness the spread of the old tree was enormous, looming twenty yards high, its top branches cutting deeply into the grey night sky. I had seen the tree in the daylight and now I tried to recall details of its appearance. Two thick trunks were joined at the base, one leaning over at a steep angle towards the river, and the yellow branches were covered by a mass of feathery, silver-green slender leaves.

Wulf rose slowly to his hands and knees. 'Stay here and do not move,' he whispered.

'You are going to leave me here?' I whined. The idea of lying alone on the river bank terrified me.

'Stay here!' he repeated irritably.

Bent almost double, Wulf started to creep noiselessly towards the tree. He seemed to be gliding over the ground. There was a dip in the bank near the tree, and as he moved into it I could just make out the hump of his back, his head and feet were out of sight.

Suddenly Wulf screamed and bounded across the ground with enormous strides, then rose and flew into the tree like a bird. I raised my head higher, trying to pierce the shroud of darkness which enveloped the tree and could just see Wulf clinging to the lowest branches, writhing and kicking. Then he screamed again, the tree erupted into a deafening explosion of cracking sounds and I saw dozens of black, screeching objects catapulted from the branches and swooping towards me like demons from hell. Gasping with terror, I scrambled backwards towards the river bank, slipping and sliding on the grass wet with night dew, and stepped into the river, crouching down on the flat rock from which I had fished earlier.

'Brand, get off that rock!' Wulf screamed. 'Get back on to the land.'

I stayed on the rock and tried to hide below the bulk of the river bank, but I saw the creatures circling over the treetops and plunging up the river towards me, their heads jutting forward like arrow-tips. Frantically I tore at my tunic, wrenched the crucifix from around my neck and held it high above my head. A tremendous gush of cold wind swept over me, my body shuddered with the rhythm of beating wings and at that instant I felt a terrific blow in the chest which hurled me bodily into the mud of the river bank. The crucifix flew from my hand and splashed into the river behind me.

Wulf appeared at my side. He gripped my head in his hands and stared into my eyes, tipping my face towards the moonlight.

'The spirits have stolen your soul!' he howled. 'You should not have stepped off the river bank. The runes cannot protect you when you are in the water. That is why you were vulnerable.'

Wulf put my left arm around his shoulders, hauled me to my feet and hustled me up the slope, past the fire-pit and into the shelter. I collapsed on my back on the pile of moss that served as my mattress.

'The web of power protected the land around the camp, but you had to step into the river!' Wulf muttered accusingly. 'The spirits are waiting for the smallest error and you did not disappoint them.'

He pulled at my tunic. 'Take this off!' he ordered.

I did as he said and sprawled back on the moss as Wulf examined my body carefully, inch by inch, by the dim light. Suddenly he stopped and pressed his forefinger into my stomach. I gasped as a searing pain shuddered through my body.

'What happened here?' Wulf demanded. He was pressing the small patch of bare skin on my stomach, where I had wiped off the paste.

'You removed some of the protective salve and your soul was stolen through that gap. It was no wonder that the spirits almost succeeded in taking your soul earlier in the evening and have now succeeded in stealing it. I gave you effective protection and you destroyed it.'

Wulf sat back on his heels and gazed at me in silence. He seemed to be trying to reach some sort of decision. I lay in silence, unable to offer any excuses or arguments.

When he spoke again, it was in a calm, quiet voice.

'You are now an empty shell, Brand. Your soul has journeyed to the spirit world. This is a special privilege, for the spirits will reveal to your soul the ways of wyrd. It has happened too soon; you are not able to be with your soul, observing all that is happening. If you can retrieve your soul, the secrets of wyrd will be yours, for the spirits will have imparted their knowledge. But if you fail to recapture your soul, your life will be extinguished like a fire in a rainstorm.'

10

HUNTING FOR AN ALLY

A BREEZE sighed softly from the river and my whole body trembled like a dry leaf. I tried to take a deep breath, but I could breathe only in short, shallow, rapid gasps and I felt as if I were going to faint. Again, I felt strangely empty inside as I had done earlier in the evening.

Wulf grasped me under the armpits and half-carried, half-dragged me to the fire-pit. I slumped against the fallen tree-trunk we used as a seat. I felt stunned and disoriented, my thoughts were confused and I was quite incapable of talking. Yet there was an important change in my state from the panic of a few moments ago; deep down within me, I knew that I would be safe with Wulf, if only I could show him that I was willing to accept the challenges he presented to me. If I could prove my worth to him, he would ensure that my encounters with his spirit-world did not kill me. I had confidence that, if necessary, Wulf could pull me from the brink of death.

The breeze blew again and I shivered uncontrollably; I felt frozen as if a winter gale were blowing bitter barbs of hail through my skin.

Wulf was moving rapidly in front of the fire-pit, piling wood on to the fire and raking it into a blaze. I pushed my freezing feet nearer the flames but could feel nothing; they were like blocks of ice.

He plunged a hand into a linen sack, dropped some herbs into two cups and poured over them hot water from the pot simmering on the hob.

'Drink it!' he ordered, sitting down next to me and staring into my face. I swivelled my gaze towards him. His eyes seemed huge in the firelight and his face looked tight and strained.

'Brand, we have to increase your life-force. Immediately! It is a matter of the utmost urgency, for you cannot survive long without your soul.'

He spoke quietly and calmly and I watched him talking, fascinated by the movement of his mouth. The words washed over me like a gentle drizzle; I could not make any sense of them.

'With your soul gone, your body will use all of your life-force to create a shadow-soul. But a shadow-soul cannot last for long: soon your body will burn itself out trying to maintain the shadow, your head will get hot, you will sweat, you will ache and within two nights you will die. Our only hope is to attempt a sudden, massive increase in your life-force so that you can project your shadow-soul into the Underworld. There, if the spirits are favourable, you will be prepared for a long journey to the spirit-world. Then, if you can summon a guardian spirit, you may be able to recapture your soul. Things could go wrong at any stage, of course, in which case you would be dead anyway.'

He paused to wipe sweat from his brow, watching me closely like a hawk. I stared straight back at him. I had just heard him pass sentence of death on me, for it was difficult even to conceive of doing all those things in two days. The chance that we would be successful in all those endeavours seemed to be non-existent.

Wulf raised his cup of herb tea to his mouth, but put it down again without drinking. He turned to look into the fire, in silence, and when he did turn back to me his eyes were moist. He spoke in a barely audible whisper:

'Of course, Brand, we may have less than two days, for your soul is journeying in the spirit-world. At any time your soul could encounter malevolent forces and be killed.'

Dimly, I pondered how a soul could be killed. Now that I had heard it put baldly, it seemed an entirely reasonable supposition.

Wulf cleared his throat and continued talking in a very quiet voice:

'I once knew a sorcerer from this forest who travelled in his soul to the spirit-world to retrieve the lost soul of a sick woman.

He laid his physical body before a fire in the spirit-house, surrounded by onlookers. Then he released his soul and began singing and chanting, describing the journey of his soul; suddenly he began to tell of dangerous spirits approaching him and as they neared him he went to meet them and tried to reason with them, but they attacked him. The sorcerer described a terrible battle, his voice hoarse with anguish, and he cried out that they had sword-ripped the belly of his soul-form. Then he fell silent.'

Wulf paused again, staring at the ground, apparently wrestling with thoughts and emotions. 'Everyone crowded forward to see if he was all right. There was an enormous wound across his stomach. Yet none of the people had touched him.'

There followed another pause before Wulf spoke again:

'The sorcerer died. He was close to me, for it was I who first introduced him to the spirit-world. But let us hope that your fate will be different.'

I could not contain myself and I burst out laughing. Wulf's story was so terrifying, so doom-laden and so final that there was nothing I could do but laugh. The forest crowded in around me and I knew now that before two nights had passed I would almost certainly be dead. I laughed long and hard, hysterically at first and then in a deeper and more releasing manner. Finally I began to relax. Death was so probable that somehow it ceased to be a threat. It was still frightening, but it was so imminent that it seemed to lose its paralysing grip on my senses. No matter what I did, I would almost certainly die and so there could be no limit to what I could do. I would fight to stay alive, but would expect to die. I laughed until tears trickled down my cheeks.

Finally Wulf grabbed my tunic and shook me to command my attention.

'Brand, listen to me. Listen! We must hunt for an ally so that we can increase your life-force thirty-fold. Tonight.'

'We are hunting tonight? In the dark?' My voice sounded loud and harsh and startled me.

'We are hunting for power. The plant is spearwort. It is a fearsome plant and can be hunted only at night when it is most vulnerable.'

I laughed again, loudly.

'How will spearwort help me?' I snorted sarcastically. 'By killing me?'

'You will have to kill spearwort first and that is no easy task,' Wulf replied coolly. 'But if you are successful we can, with the help of spearwort, project your shadow-soul from your body like a luminous personal spirit. Then you will be able to journey to the Underworld, where the mighty smiths of magic will prepare you to journey to the spirit-world.'

I shrugged my shoulders to indicate that I had no objections to a night-time hunt. Since I was doomed to die in any case, everything seemed possible.

Wulf opened his hands and began to pass them over my body close to my tunic but without touching me. He seemed to be feeling for something with his palms and I was suddenly reminded of his cure of the horse at Cydda's farm. He nodded, apparently in satisfaction.

'The shadow-soul is breathing out your shield-skin, preventing your body from crumbling and keeping it alive. But it cannot continue for long. We have no time to lose. Come on!'

Wulf began to make preparations to leave. My fingers still trembled with cold, but I realised that my body was no longer numb and frozen. Unsteadily I strapped on my shoes, wrapped my cloak around me and as soon as we were ready, Wulf led the way from the clearing and northwards along the river bank, setting a slow pace, allowing me to stay close behind him.

A pale moon glowed intermittently between drifting clouds, and shimmered through the forest canopy like silver star-dust. Shrubbery winked and rustled as we pushed past and the soft ground-cover wriggled under my feet. At first I had difficulty walking; I felt as if my body were pivoted at the navel and my feet were slipping about on ice. Gradually I gained control of my balance and concentrated on treading close behind Wulf. Suddenly he stopped and I walked straight into the back of him.

'Be careful!' he hissed. 'Now listen. Spearwort is an extremely powerful and dangerous force. It will be expecting us and as soon as it knows we are coming, it will lay a trap. It will send forces after us.'

He paused and glanced at the tree cover at the back of the clearing. Then he whispered into my ear:

'We must hunt in absolute silence. When we reach the plant, try not to look at it directly for it has been known to kill with a look of power. Keep your gaze to one side of the spearwort and watch it out of the corner of your eye. You must try to get as close as you can to the plant, moving so slowly that it cannot even detect that you *are* moving. I shall give you my knife. When you are within two or three paces, leap in and plunge the knife as deeply as possible into the ground at the base of the plant.'

Wulf pulled his head back and regarded me steadily.

I nodded, stiffly. 'How will I know which plant?'

'You will know. But remember, if spearwort suspects our presence too early, it could kill. Under no circumstances must you talk. Spearwort will not give you a second chance. You are hunting – but remember, you are also being hunted.'

We resumed walking and, after a time, Wulf led us across a shallow ford in the river and we waded through the swift, cold current, swirling past our feet like some slithering animal pulling at our ankles. On the opposite bank we plunged into thicker woodland and the tree cover blotted out the moon. As we pushed through the undergrowth I sensed the presence of larger animals and once glimpsed the bulk of a bear watching us from a slight rise, behind a clutter of bramble and low branches. Wolves howled in the distance, foxes' eyes glistened from hiding places and the undergrowth was alive with badgers scurrying for cover.

As the forest became more thickly wooded, our path twisted and turned around trees and shrubbery huddled together like children in darkness, and soon my face stung from the lashing of low branches. Wulf pushed on ahead of me. Suddenly I realised that I could no longer hear the swish of his legs through the undergrowth. I stopped in my tracks and listened carefully, sweat running salty into my mouth, but I could hear nothing. I peered blindly into the surrounding shrubbery, but he was gone. Panic pounded in my chest and I stood rigidly like a trapped rabbit, trying to decide what to do. Then my heart leapt into my mouth: I heard Wulf's voice. I knew that something must be terribly wrong, for he had insisted on total silence. I turned and looked behind me. The low branches that I had pushed aside had closed behind me, blocking my view. I held my breath and listened hard. Wulf spoke again, this time from my right.

'I am on the other side of the hawthorn. Can you come through?'

Quickly I scanned the bushes. Just ahead of me the red berries of a hawthorn gleamed like black stones in the darkness. I dropped to my hands and knees and crawled through a space near the base of the bush. To my relief, the familiar silhouette of Wulf's cloak and hat loomed ahead of me. He had his back to me and seemed to be examining something in the trees to his left. I scrambled out from under the hawthorn and stood next to him, peering in the direction of his gaze.

'What's wrong, Wulf?' I whispered.

He did not reply, but continued to look away from me as if observing something in the trees. I tried to attract his attention again:

'Wulf, why did you speak?'

Slowly he turned towards me, his face shrouded by the broad brim of his hat. As his gaze met mine, I went cold with horror; the face was grotesque, with eyes white and blank like stream pebbles and a black mouth opening and closing silently. I could not move or even tear my eyes away from the horrible face; it was like being trapped in a terrible nightmare. Then I heard a high-pitched whine and felt a tremendous pressure inside my head. Desperately I struggled to move away, but my feet were rooted to the spot. I was aware of the demon's hand reaching towards me, and suddenly I recoiled from a mighty blow which lifted me right into the air and hurled me through the bushes to crash into the undergrowth. I rolled over on my back, staring panic-stricken at the mass of waving and spinning branches, losing all sense of direction. Then the bramble branches parted and the shadowy figure came towards me. Frantically I averted my face and tried to scramble out from under the shrub, kicking and flailing my arms wildly, but strong hands held me fast, gripped my head and slowly forced me to look back into the face. In a frenzy of terror I closed my eyes and screamed. When I opened them again, the face had changed – it loomed close still, but I was looking into the eyes of Wulf.

He helped me to my feet. I could breathe only in sobs and I was trembling uncontrollably. My entire body ached as if I had taken a terrible beating.

He put an arm around my shoulders and helped me from the thickets into a clearing under a large beech tree, where I slumped to the ground and sat with my head between my knees. Wulf squatted next to me. Neither of us spoke. I knew I had made a terrible mistake and Wulf had rescued me. My physical fatigue had interrupted my concentration and when I heard the voice I should have gone in the opposite direction.

I sat for a long time and Wulf made no effort to foreshorten my recovery period. Eventually I began to regain control of my trembling limbs.

'What happened?' Wulf said eventually, keeping his voice low.

In a whisper I tried to describe what I thought had occurred and Wulf nodded.

'Spearwort is a cunning force. It lured you into a trap. If I had not returned to look for you, it might have killed you. You are very lucky, Brand.'

Wulf stood and looked into the shadowy forest in all directions, then motioned me to get to my feet.

'This time, stay alert,' he warned. 'Spearwort may try again. No talking. Stay close to me.'

Wulf set off into the woods at a slower pace and I clung to him like thatch moss. Every animal sound and movement now seethed with threat and I stayed alert and vigilant.

After a short distance, Wulf stopped abruptly. I could not see his face but I could hear him sniffing. I breathed in deeply; I could smell only the sweet coolness of the forest. Suddenly Wulf left the trail and made off at an angle to the right, walking in a crouch; I doubled over and stayed as close to him as possible. At one point I got my foot caught in matted ferns and had to resist the temptation to hang on to his cloak to avoid losing him.

Twenty paces into the undergrowth, Wulf stopped in front of a large shrub. I looked up at its black bulk and recognised the outline of a dog-rose, clusters of pink flowers looking like small faces in the shadows. Wulf dropped on to his hands and knees and peered cautiously between the lower branches. I squatted close to him, glancing nervously behind me.

Wulf eased himself forward on to his stomach and slithered through a small gap at the base of the shrub. For a moment I was alone in the darkness and in near panic I scrambled through the gap after him. He was crouching on the other side of the shrub, facing a small clearing. Carefully I crawled out of the shrub and rested next to him. Immediately I became aware of something strange about his posture, something that I sensed rather than saw; he seemed to be frozen into a half-bending, half-squatting position, staring at the trunk of a small tree. I focused my eyes in the direction in which he was looking and could just make out the trunk of an aspen. Almost immediately I felt a hot tingling sensation on my left cheek, as if I were sitting too close to a fire. I turned my head to the left and was met by the piercing stare of numerous gleaming, yellow eyes. I tried to see some detail of spearwort's appearance, but I could take in only the cold stare of the yellow eyes. My body tensed with alarm and I jerked back my head to look at Wulf; he remained stock-still, staring at the tree. I remembered that he had warned me to avoid the direct gaze of the spearwort. I looked at the tree, but still had to shift my gaze to the right to avoid the glare.

Wulf started to move again in the same strange, slow manner. He glided stiffly and silently towards the yellow-eyed plants, his head averted, staring at a space two or three paces to the right of them. I tried to follow him, but my calf muscles were so tense that I had to roll forward to take some weight off my legs. At the same time I became aware that I had been holding my breath. I sucked in two long, silent breaths; the air in the clearing smelled sour and oppressive. I crawled across the clearing, Wulf a few feet ahead of me, still moving almost imperceptibly towards the plants. As I watched him, his right arm glided behind his back and his knife slipped silently into his hand. I wiped my sweating palm on my cloak, reached out and took the weapon. With a wave of his hand, Wulf motioned me past him towards the plant. I swallowed hard, moving forward very slowly like a man swimming under water in a deep pool. I moved to within three paces of the spearwort. Suddenly a horrible, low moan came from the eyes, and I froze in mid-stride.

'Kill!' Wulf screamed.

I shot forward, the knife flashed and plunged and the yellow eyes shuddered and reared back like an adder about to strike.

'Run!' Wulf yelled, sprinting past me to the dog-rose. I lurched after him, pursued by the low moaning and dived through the shrub, shutting my eyes against the slashing branches. Scrabbling desperately at loose soil, I catapulted myself out through the other side. Wulf was waiting for me and as I tried to get up to run, he pushed me down to the ground and held me there, signalling vigorously for me to keep still. He put his mouth near my ear and whispered:

'When I tell you, go up slowly to the plant and dig it out with your fingers, making a ditch a hand's-breadth from the stem. Pull out the whole root, with the knife still buried in it.'

Wulf put a finger to his lips and indicated that we were to sit in silence.

We waited for an age, Wulf squatting next to the dog-rose and periodically peering through the branches. Eventually he signalled with a jerk of his head that we were to re-enter the clearing.

He crawled under the wild rose and I followed close behind. As soon as I emerged into the clearing, the moaning again filled my ears in rhythmic bursts. The sound grew louder and I began to shiver as if caught in a biting wind. I pulled my cloak closer around me and stared at Wulf, hoping desperately for a signal to run, but he motioned for me to approach the plant.

Heart pounding, I slowly uncurled from my crouch, rolled forward on the balls of my feet and crept towards the spearwort. Gradually the moaning died away to a whisper. From close up I saw that the yellow eyes were a tight array of petals in a daisy-like formation. The knife looked thick, solid, and deadly, buried to the hilt in the ground at the base of the plant.

With my fingers I began to work loose the soil around the base of the stem, avoiding the knife. The night wind crept around the clearing and sighed through the trees above us. In the distance an owl hooted: a melancholy, mournful call. Wulf remained behind me, squatting absolutely motionless.

Gradually I created a ditch surrounding the plant, about as deep as my hand and a hand's breadth from the stem. Then I burrowed my hands beneath the root, as we had done days earlier when collecting plants on the plateau. I stood slowly, and lifted the plant cleanly from the ground. Wulf leaned over and gently brushed away excess soil; the root glistened wet and white, shining throught the darkness. It was dark and swollen, with a split on either side of the intruding blade.

Wulf took my arm and we began to back out of the clearing. His head swivelled from side to side, apparently scanning other spearwort plants further back under the trees. We crawled under the dog-rose, and Wulf took the plant from me. My hands tingled where I had held the wet root and I tried to wipe them dry on the grass.

Now Wulf took a linen sack from his belt, spread it on the ground and placed the plant on it with the root at the centre. The point of the knife blade protruded a few inches from the bottom of the root. Carefully, Wulf wrapped the bag around the root and then gave it back to me.

'Take good care of it,' he whispered. 'It gave you trouble earlier, but now that you have captured it, spearwort will be a powerful ally.'

I followed Wulf back through the forest, cradling the plant protectively in the crook of my arm. It felt heavy and strong, like a small, adult hunting animal. As we talked, I began to feel stronger. The chill left me and soon I was sweating under the heavy cloak. My thoughts came clearer and for a time I thought my soul had returned of its own accord. But occasionally the ominous feeling of emptiness returned to my body and I knew that my time was still diminishing rapidly.

We retraced our route along the river and eventually emerged on to the grassy bank of our camp. The fire was almost dead, so Wulf immediately set to work to save it, blowing into the embers and placing dry kindling carefully on the hottest part. I put the bundle containing the spearwort on the ground near the fire-pit and watched Wulf work.

In a short while the fire was healthy again. Wulf took the linen sack to a spot very near the stone perimeter of the pit and unwrapped it gently. When I saw the plant I was shocked. The large root had shrunk amazingly and the yellow eye lay pale and blind on the sacking, a withered flower connected to the root by a flaccid stem.

Wulf settled into a crouching position next to the plant and motioned for me to do the same. I felt drained and exhausted, but not at all sleepy. I sat opposite Wulf and we watched the plant for hours. I was totally riveted by the white root as, through the night, it curled up gradually in a desperate attempt to accommodate the cruel bulk of the blade. Life ebbed out of the spearwort slowly.

Occasionally my thoughts would wander and linger over events recent or long ago. The faces and voices of people dear to me drifted in and out, each as clear and bright as candle-flame. But always my attention returned to the spearwort, my ally, lying at my feet.

After a time, the night wind died down to a murmur and the sky streaked with dawn light. Suddenly the clearing around us took on an eerie luminosity; the spearwort eye seemed momentarily to glow brilliant yellow, then faded completely. Wulf placed his hand on the dead root and carefully withdrew the knife. I felt a tightness in my throat and hot tears coursed down my cheeks as if we had conducted a vigil over a dying friend.

Wulf gathered the shrunken root in his hands, carried it to the river bank and immersed it in the water. He scraped lichen from a rock near the bank and packed it in clumps on the wet spearwort root. Then he collected and filled our two cooking pots with river water and dropped the spearwort into one of them. We returned to the fire-pit. There Wulf placed the spearwort pot on to the stones at the back of the fire, where it would receive gentle heat. He filled the other pot with vegetables from our store and put it on the fire. When they were cooked, we broke our fast.

11

THE CAULDRON OF POWER

THE SUN rose slowly over the horizon into a pale blue sky streaked with thin wisps of cloud, like torn lace drifting high on the wind. I sat hunched against a tree on the edge of our camp, brooding blackly. Since dawn's first light, in the quiet time before daybreak, my mood had plunged from exhilaration to despair. After we had eaten, Wulf had gone to walk alone in the forest and I had been left to my thoughts. Gradually I had become increasingly obsessed by my loss of the crucifix which had been knocked from my hand into the river by the same spirits who had stolen my soul. The Lord's presence was not diminished, of course, for He watches over his flock always. But the crucifix was my tangible link with the Mission and especially Eappa, who had presented it to me. And I knew that this day might be my last. Wulf had predicted two nights of life at the most and we had spent one of them searching for spearwort. After the exertions of the spearwort hunt I now felt weak and lethargic and a dull ache set in behind my eyes. If I was to die this night, I wished to go to the Lord with the comfort of my crucifix.

As I tipped my head back, trying to ease the ache in my head, I noticed a lone hawk gliding high on the wind, barely a speck against the blue sky. Idly I wondered what unsuspecting creature would become the hawk's next victim and share with me the same last day of life.

As soon as the early morning light turned from grey to silver, I went down to the river to look for the crucifix. I felt very light-headed and as I picked my way down the river bank I slipped and stumbled repeatedly. The water was cold and clear and I paddled down river as far as the bend, examining every inch of the river bed within a foot of the bank. Then I tracked up and down the river, further and further from the bank, until I was submerged to the waist and could no longer see the bottom. There was no sign of the precious cross.

Finally, feet numbed by the cold water, I climbed on to the bank and walked dejectedly towards the shelter. I felt exhausted, and twice I almost fell before I reached the camp. Wulf was squatting near the fire-pit, shredding plants with his knife and dropping fragments into the spearwort mixture which simmered slowly on the back of the hob. He looked up as I approached.

'How do you feel?' he said cheerfully.

'Fine,' I replied, my voice betraying the lie, as I sat down next to him.

'Wulf, I can't find my crucifix.'

'Spearwort is doing well,' he said, jabbing his knife towards the pot on the hob. I struggled up to look into the pot and saw the dark green spearwort preparation bubbling and churning. Dutifully I raised a smile of approval before collapsing again. I was no longer interested in spearwort. In the clear light of morning, I did not see how a wizened plant could remove the dreadful feeling of emptiness from my chest and restore my missing soul. I wanted only the comfort of the crucifix.

'I can't find my crucifix,' I said again, irritably. 'I have searched the river bed as deep as I can go and down river as far as the bend. Wulf, I don't want to die without my crucifix.'

Wulf stopped working, hesitated, then put down his knife and walked around the fire-pit towards me. He crouched by my side and scrutinised me in silence. His eyes were bright and piercing and I dropped my gaze to look away towards the trees. I found his stare disturbing; whenever he looked directly into my eyes he seemed to see into my heart.

'Brand, you are shortly to be journeying to the Underworld, where you will see things never even dreamed of by your masters. After that, I hope you will be able to summon a guardian spirit who will take you to the spirit-world. If we fail and death takes you, then so be it. But do not plan for death as if the terror of it could thereby be avoided. Accept death as part of life, and live for life only. Think of the tasks you need to perform before the next night is over and do not waste your energies worrying about a bronze amulet.'

I listened to him with a kind of detached interest. The events of the night, the attack by the creature I had mistakenly identified as Wulf, the emotional witness of the death of the spearwort plant, the failure to find my crucifix – all had left me feeling drained. I felt weak and shivery and I knew that I was sickening rapidly. I wished that I had the crucifix for comfort.

'We have to prepare two wildfires,' Wulf said loudly. When I heard him, I realised that it was at least the second time he had repeated the phrase. I nodded slowly. Wulf grasped me by the wrist and pulled me to my feet. As he stared into my eyes from very close, our noses almost touched.

'Brand, you have used almost all your life-force in hunting and capturing spearwort.'

My attention had slipped and he grabbed my hair and held my gaze steady.

'You must help me to make wildfire. It is essential that you participate in building it, even though you do the simplest tasks.'

He looked at the sky and then at the trees, measuring the morning shadow.

'It is time to work,' he said. 'Collect some dry kindling from the hazels.'

He pointed down river to a hazel coppice close to the bank. I pulled myself resignedly to my feet, trudged along the river bank to the coppice and laboriously collected an armful of brittle twigs. By the time I returned to the shelter, Wulf was kneeling on the grass near the river bank; lying next to him were two pieces of oak branch, each about a yard long, and an enormous heap of freshly picked, spiky-leaved plants.

'Select the smallest kindling and pile it there,' he instructed, pointing to an area about half-way between the river bank and the fire-pit. Then he stood up, strode to the river and waded knee-deep into the water. As I watched him, he bent over and dipped his arms into the water up to his shoulders, pulled up stones from the river-bed, examined them closely and then appeared to replace them in their original position.

Puzzled, I turned to my task, sorting through the pile of

kindling, selecting the thinnest pieces and testing them for dryness. It took me a very long time. I had just finished stacking the best wood when Wulf splashed on to the bank carrying two fist-sized stones. He dried them carefully on his tunic and then laid them on the grass. One stone was flat and disc-shaped, the other more rounded and larger at one end, like a pear. I sat down and watched him.

Wulf waded back into the water and pulled on to the bank a large, flinty boulder. He rolled it on the grass to remove excess water, then set it down near the small stones. Picking up one of the oak stakes, he stripped off some of the bark and tested the wood by digging in his thumbnail. Grunting approval, he placed the disc-shaped stone flat on the ground in front of him and laid the small oak stake across it. With the point of his knife he pierced the oak stake near one end, then twisted the knife point until he had cut a deep, narrow impression half-way through the thickness of the wood. Rolling the stake over, he pushed in the knife at a point corresponding exactly to the hole he had made on the first side, and drilled a small hole right through the wood. Then he stood the piece of wood up on the stone, with the hole towards the top of the stake and sharpened the bottom end to a point.

All his preparations were carried out with exquisite sureness and control and I watched him in absolute fascination.

Wulf turned his attention back to the oak stake, pushing the point of the oak into the soft ground in the centre of my small pile of kindling. Standing with his feet astride, he used the large rock to hammer the stake into the ground. About a third of its length sank into the soft turf. Wulf tested it: the stake stood solidly. Finally he used his knife to clean the top of the oak stake where it had been crushed and split by the impact of the rock.

When he had finished preparing the stake, Wulf sorted through the pile of kindling I had collected and pulled out a long, thin hazel wand. Tucking it under his armpit, he scraped the bark from it, working carefully – presumably to avoid snapping the dry wood. When he had finished, he filled his right palm with a few of the bright green leaves, placed the hazel wand over them, closed his fist and rubbed the leaves vigorously back and forth along the full length of the stripped wood. The crushed leaves covered the stick with a dark and shiny juice. Wulf then carefully inserted the gleaming hazel wand into the hole he had drilled through the oak stake, but the fit was too tight. Gently, he gouged the knife into the oak stake and slightly increased the diameter of the hole. Then he fed the hazel wand into it and pushed it slowly forwards and backwards. There was just sufficient room for the wand to pass through the hole. Gradually Wulf increased his speed until his hand was a blur as he whipped the wand back and forth, and after a time, wisps of smoke escaped from the hole. Both pieces of wood glowed red and tiny chips of spark floated down on to the kindling and died. Immediately Wulf tore the willow wand from the hole and plunged it into the dry kindling. It smouldered. Putting his face close to the kindling, he blew in long and steady breaths until it glowed, smoked and then burned.

Wulf collapsed back on his haunches, his chest heaving up and down. Sweat trickled down his face and dripped from his chin.

'This is wildfire,' he wheezed. 'Wood on wood, built from the substance it consumes.'

Rapidly Wulf built up the fire until it cracked and popped and, fed by the breath of the early morning breeze, shot showers of sparks high into the air. He stopped for a moment to get his breath, then turned to me.

'In order to journey to the spirits, the sorcerer has to be a human firefly, lighting his own way through the darkness of other worlds,' he said. 'Your life-force is your wildfire, your inner fire. It will enable you to project your shadow-soul to the Underworld, where you shall be prepared for your journey into the spirit-world.'

Wulf made another small pile of kindling on the grass, several feet from the first so that the two were parallel with the bank of the river. He lit it with a burning brand from the first wildfire and it crackled hungrily into the kindling, spitting sparks and flames. Wulf then took me by the arm and gestured for me to sit between the fires: I crawled across the grass and slumped in the space between the groups of small, crackling flames. In the open space the morning breeze blew cool, but sunlight crept through the trees and lay dappled on my skin; I watched the tiny patches of light moving in the breeze on my arms which were still green from Wulf's protective salve.

'Drink some of this.' Wulf's voice broke into my reverie, and I looked up at him. He placed a mug in my hand and curled my fingers round it.

'I have boiled the spearwort and it is ready for you to drink. When you have drunk all of it, your life-force will be increased thirty-fold: enough to propel your shadow-soul from your body and into the cauldron of the Underworld.'

'Drink,' he said, gesturing towards the cup. 'It will ignite your inner fire.'

I began to laugh nervously. 'What will it do, Wulf? Make flames in my stomach?'

'You will feel nothing at first. Drink it,' he urged.

I sipped cautiously at the steaming liquid and to my surprise it tasted quite refreshing, rather like lemon balm tea.

The sun had now risen well above the trees and began to beam down strongly. Wulf built up the two fires and soon I was hot and parched. Again Wulf dipped the mug into the spearwort pot and I gulped the hot drink thirstily. This time the spearwort tasted stronger, with a musty and faintly bitter after-taste. Wulf sat on the ground in front of me and took the mug when I had finished drinking.

'When you increase your life-force, you develop great inner power,' he said. 'There are many ways to develop this power using your own resources, but we are forced to work with the greatest urgency and so we are enlisting the aid of spearwort as an ally. Spearwort will vastly increase your inner fire. And when you sit between two wildfires, you enter a vast cauldron of forces flowing through you like the wind. Changes in power within you are reflected by changes outside you, for all the patterns of wyrd are present in the body in the same way as they are present in the sun, moon and stars.'

I was having great difficulty in following what Wulf was saying. He was staring into my face, his eyes holding my attention for fleeting moments before my attention wandered. His voice broke in and out of my thoughts along with the chirp and chatter of the birds in the trees. In between, my mind again pictured episodes from my childhood like reflections in a still pool; flat, silent, but accurate in every detail.

Wulf left me for a time, though I occasionally glimpsed him piling more wood on to the fires. I took off my tunic and then my shoes, and sat naked on the grass, tasting the salt of sweat running into my mouth and feeling it trickling down the inside of my arms.

When the sun had climbed high in the sky, Wulf returned and crouched in front of me, examining my eyes carefully. Then he placed his palms on my forehead and the back of my neck. I could feel the heat in my head pulsing against his cool hands. He felt down the entire length of my spine with his fingers, taking plenty of time, pressing at various points on my back.

His eyes were sparkling, his white teeth bared in a broad grin. 'You are doing well, Brand. Your life-force is now increased ten-fold. Soon your cauldron of power will be boiling over and pulsing along your fibres. This is where lies the power of the sorcerer: the ability to control the source of inner life-force, and raise the level to such an extent that power radiates along his fibres and throughout the web of wyrd. If you can generate enough power you will be able to project your shadow-soul along your fibres and into the Underworld, where your fibres will be re-woven like a pattern-welded blade. The magical smiths of the Underworld fire the swords and knives of sorcery by transmuting Mother Earth's metals in the flames of wildfire. Likewise they will forge your fibres in the cauldron of your own inner fire.'

Wulf piled more wood on to the fires, building them higher and hotter. I drank two more cups of spearwort, which now tasted stronger and more bitter than before. For a time I felt sick and faint. Jumbles of thoughts and memories, especially incidents from my childhood, drifted repeatedly through my mind like autumn leaves on a stream. Images from childhood dreams floated in front of my eyes and disembodied voices from years ago, including my own, sounded inside my head. Eventually I seemed to sleep. I awoke at one point, briefly, feeling much better. I had surging spasms down my back which at first I took to be aching muscles from sitting so long, but when I concentrated my attention on the sensations I realised that they felt like tiny droplets of heat trickling down my backbone. I slipped back into sleep.

When I awoke again I was sitting bolt upright. My head felt as if it would burst, full of heat and fire, my spine charged with surging heat, my fingers tingling, legs throbbing. I experienced a tremendous sensation of power and strength, as if I could have leaped to my feet and uprooted the nearest oak.

Wulf materialised at my side.

'Your wildfire is melting the ice-bonds of your shield-skin,' he said. His voice seemed to tremble, whether with excitement or urgency I could not tell. 'In continuously breathing out our skin-shield, we thereby clamp our soul in layers of confinement; layers which define our existence but enslave our souls.'

He reached out and patted my face gently. 'The ice of your shield-skin is dripping off your chin,' he said.

I wiped my face with my palms. My face was drenched with sweat and my soaked hair lay matted flat against my scalp.

'The shield-skin clamps our soul like the bonds of frost,' he murmured. 'The heat of your inner cauldron must be stoked to such a level that the frost melts. Just as a snake cannot grow until it sheds its skin, so you cannot extend your soul until you shed the restrictions of your shield-skin.'

I sat and sweated until the sun sank behind the horizon and the wildfires on each side of me seemed like twin, earth-bound suns, lighting up the whole clearing with their brilliance. Flurries of moths, attracted by the flames, wheeled and dived about in the smoke. At the bottom of the slope the river surged past, silenced by the crackle of the flames, reflecting the firelight like a river of blood.

At one instant Wulf appeared in front of me silhouetted against a sky glowing with an orange sunset, but when I looked again he was lit instead by the flicker of flame from the wildfires; more time had passed and the sky behind him was dark with night. Wulf strode to my side, knelt down and placed his hand on my stomach. I shuddered at his touch, my skin alive and sensitive.

'Air is the fan of wildfire, breath is the fan of inner fire,' he whispered. 'Make your breathing deeper and slower.'

As soon as I heard his instructions, I realised that I was breathing in short, shallow gasps. I took in a deep breath, my ears hummed and whistled and the pressure mounted inside my head. Wulf passed me one more cup of spearwort and squatted in front of me, watching every movement as I sipped the drink. I still had the sensation of tremendous power, but I no longer wanted to get up and exert physical effort; I was rooted to the spot and had no desire to move.

Gradually, as I breathed deeply, I began to feel very relaxed. My breathing slowed further and I suddenly realised I was having difficulty keeping my eyes fixed on Wulf's face. My tongue started flicking in and out like a lizard; it buzzed and tingled, then went numb. I could not control the sensations, yet I felt certain that I *could* assert control if I really wished. But I did not attempt to stop any part of the process now; I would do whatever Wulf instructed. My life depended on it.

Abruptly Wulf floated out of focus and my eyes closed involuntarily. I felt buoyant, as though floating on water. Then my head felt so light that it seemed to want to come away from my body. Suddenly I began to separate. I appeared to move out of my body and to be sitting about two feet above my right shoulder, looking down at my head. I was too astonished to be frightened, but when I tried to move my eyes flickered open again and I was back inside my body. I looked for Wulf, but he was not there. I tried to call to him, but my tongue lay limp and helpless on the floor of my mouth.

Just then Wulf came back into vision, sitting squarely on the spot where I had just seen him.

'Rock back and forth.' His voice rumbled, as though it came from underground.

Slowly I inched my body backwards, then leaned forward very carefully, but I felt as if I were perched on top of a mountain and any movement would plunge me into an abyss.

'Rock!' Wulf repeated sternly. 'You now possess enough life-force to enable your shadow-soul to slip out through your shield-skin. Relax, and allow your shield-skin to move aside. Give yourself some space through which to escape.'

I tried to rock back and forth but my body became rigid with fear. I felt sure that I would fall.

'Brand, you are afraid because inside your shield-skin you feel soft and vulnerable. You are like a tortoise in its shell. But you need not be afraid; you will remove only one layer of shield-skin, escape temporarily and then return to your body. And for each layer of shield-skin removed, you will gain a guardian spirit. Some sorcerers have as many as nine guardians, but one is sufficient for you to journey to the spirit-world.

'Now, rock; let your shadow-soul out of your body. It knows where to go.'

I tried it again and this time I was able to set up a very slight rocking motion. I felt sure that I would fall, but I was determined to let it happen. I rocked a little further each time. Suddenly I pitched forward out of control, my body trembled violently and I felt myself floating out. I shut my eyes tightly and let it happen. I knew that I was journeying to the Underworld.

12

THE DWARF OF THE UNDERWORLD

WHEN I OPENED my eyes I was plunging frantically along a narrow deer track, face slashed and whipped by low branches, pursued by something monstrous. Its hot, rancid breath burned my neck and desperately I kicked my legs out harder; but the ground was soft and spongy and I could get no grip. My legs felt like fast-melting candles and my strides chopped shorter and shorter. Whining with terror, I scrambled across a small dark clearing and staggered towards a gap in the bushes on the far side. A rush of familiar smells sucked me towards a small rise at the base of a gigantic beech, where a hole lay invisible in the darkness; without hesitation I dived into its dark, safe confines.

Suddenly I was suffocating. I forced my head back, gulping for air like a landed fish. I was trapped in a long, dark tunnel, a tiny, distant, bright circle of light glimmering at the far end. I struggled and kicked for air, but the life was being crushed from my chest. Just when I thought I would surely die, the walls of the tunnel pulsed and surged, and I slid smoothly down the darkness towards the circle of light. The walls stopped moving and I was stuck ten feet from the end of the tunnel, my arms still pinned to my side but able now to breathe. Kicking and squirming, I managed to worm my way down the passage inch by inch until I reached the end, thrust my face into the light, and immediately recoiled from tremendous crashing sounds ringing out rhythmically like hammers on metal in some gigantic smithy. Pushing forward again, I blinked into the brightness to see a huge cave stretching away into the distance, the whole cavernous space flooded with a diffuse orange light. Immense daggers of rock hung from the ceiling and others reached up from the floor, like the teeth of some monstrous dragon. Still stuck in the mouth of the tunnel, I swivelled my eyes and saw the floor of the enormous cave glowing like molten gold. Smoke from some hidden source gushed and hissed towards the roof and I thought I must surely be in the bowels of hell.

Suddenly all light was blocked out by the monstrous figure of a gigantic man, huge but built like a dwarf, his naked body stubby but muscular as if forcibly restrained from growing. His head moved towards me: huge, flaring nostrils and small glassy eyes, smooth like river pebbles. I remembered the eyes of the creature who had attacked me on the night of the spearwort hunt, and I struggled violently to retreat back into the tunnel. I tried to scream, but I could not expand my chest sufficiently to draw breath; all I managed was a gurgling whimper.

I struggled again and the face moved away from me, to be replaced by an enormous hand holding an outsized pair of metal fire tongs. A sharp stab of pain gripped my neck and coursed through my body and with one gigantic heave of the fire tongs, the monster pulled me into the cave. I crumpled on to the floor like a rag doll, my body pushed out of shape by the narrow tunnel.

The face bent over and peered at me again, then the dwarf turned and stumped away.

For a time I lay motionless, hardly daring to move. Eventually I raised my head and peered down the cave. For a moment it looked eerily small and cramped as if I were peering into a rabbits' burrow; then it was huge and bright once more.

The dwarf seemed to be at least a hundred paces away, tiny now; I saw two others behind him, equally small, pumping something up and down, and I heard the hiss of distant bellows. Immediately the orange light became more intense. I knew now that the huge cavern was some kind of underground smithy and Wulf's words roared back into my mind: he had forewarned that I would be 'prepared' by the dwarf smiths of the Underworld, magical dealers in wildfire.

The sight of the dwarf frightened me, yet I felt a strange sense of destiny as if I had been meant for this experience from the moment I was born. I had never even conceived of such a place as this cave, yet now that I was here I felt as if it was right, as if I belonged.

I rolled slowly into a crouching position and watched the first dwarf cracking a hammer down repeatedly on to a long, thin piece of glowing metal resting on an anvil – showering sparks, turning the metal deftly this way and that, always placing it precisely to meet the rhythmic drop of the hammer.

The smith plunged the red-hot strip of metal into a huge cauldron of water and a tremendous gush of steam hissed to the ceiling. Suddenly he turned and stumped across the floor towards me with a tight, strangely constricted gait, and as he neared me he seemed to grow in proportion to the giant shadows he cast on the cave walls. He reached out a massive hand and gripped me. I squeaked with pain, but could do nothing. His arms had grown so that they were as thick as oak trunks and his mighty fist clamped my entire body, pinning my arms to my sides. He lifted me up high into the air, brought me close to his eyes and then he spoke:

'All-Wise I am called: I dwell under Middle-Earth, in the rocks of the Underworld. I am a dwarf in the world of giants and a smith firing the secrets of sorcery.'

His voice was strangely and eerily beautiful and melodious, like the gentle rumble of an underground stream.

'Declare your name,' he said, more an invitation than a command.

I tried to speak, but could say nothing.

'Have you runes?' he rumbled, raising eyebrows thick as black sheep.

I nodded weakly. I was terrified, yet I did not panic for I knew that he would not harm me.

Opening his hand, the giant dwarf held me in his palm like a trembling butterfly. I reached awkwardly into my tunic and pulled out the rune-stick. He took it, the stick tiny in his fingers, and read it out loud in words I did not understand. Then he carried me to his furnace and laid me gently on my back on a flat slab of rock, next to a mighty, black anvil of traditional shape but enormous proportions. The anvil was mounted on a gigantic slab of oak.

I swivelled my head to look past the anvil towards the fire. At least eight cauldrons seethed on top of the fire, the basin-shaped bottoms glowing red, and pillars of steam rose from their mouths to gather in the murky shadows of the cave roof.

The dwarf spoke again:

'This is a sorcerer's smithy, miles deep, where webs of wyrd are welded. Your runes are strong and call for urgent powers to recover a captured soul.'

Dimly, in the back of my mind, I puzzled over the fact that Wulf had cut the runes long before the spirits had captured my soul; but I no longer questioned such events. That much, at least, I had learned.

The smith spoke again: 'You are a far-wanderer, traversing forests in the service of your god. It is the will of the spirits that you enter the realms of wyrd. I shall re-pattern your fibres, so that you may journey with a guardian into the world of spirits with the strength and vision of a sorcerer.'

He gestured towards the furnace.

'Each of these cauldrons, hard-hammered in the heat of wyrd, will reveal powers. It is then your task to become aware of the secrets welded within you.'

The smith reached into the nearest steaming cauldron and pulled out the piece of metal he had hammered. It dripped and gleamed, two razor-sharp edges winking in the strange light, a long knife of such beauty and elegance as I had never seen before. My eyes were held in thrall by the blade, fascinated by the handle of horn he slid on to the hilt.

Suddenly the dwarf snatched me from the slab, I saw the knife flash and instantaneously I flew to the roof of the cave like a stone from a catapult. Floating high against the roof of rock, I had the incredible sensation of being in a body still, but a body without substance: my being seemed indistinguishable from the steam which swirled around me like a winter fog. For an instant the engulfing steam cleared and I glimpsed myself far below – or rather, I glimpsed my body lying still on the slab of rock. My mind registered terror but I felt no grip of emotion; only an acceptance, a resignation, a sense of helplessness. Steam poured across my vision and then cleared again; the body far below looked familiar and complete, yet strangely sparkling and iridescent.

Then the dwarf grasped the body and lifted it from the slab. The great knife slashed again and I gasped in wonder; he had sliced my body free from a mass of shimmering fibres and then cut it into pieces, flinging the parts into the various cauldrons boiling furiously on the fire.

I felt no pain, only the shock of the spectacle I was witnessing. The network of light that lay on the slab, conforming still to the shape of my body, was a wondrous sight. Running down the entire length of the spine was a strip of intense blue light; as I looked closer through the shifting curtain of mist, I could see that this light was a length of moving liquid webbing and that woven across and spraying out from the spine were countless more fibres – brilliant slivers of light, waving slowly like the white heads of seeding dandelions blown by a gentle breeze. Spasms of yellow or orange light pulsated along the blue spine, beating rhythmically like blood in a vein and spinning whirlpools of sparkling fibres bright as stars in a winter sky.

Steam blinded me again and I floated across the roof of the cave, drifting past the massive icicles of rock, until I could again see the dwarfs, the image undulating through the steam like an under-water scene.

I saw the dwarf take the pieces of my body one by one from the cauldrons; first my head was picked out and pounded on the anvil; I winced as the heavy hammer crashed, but could feel no pain. The furnace was roaring now with the pumping bellows of the other two dwarfs, and the smith plucked from the fire a strip of white hot metal and forged something into my head. Then he seemed to take out the eyes and to do something to them with the strip of metal before putting them back. Again I felt a strange combination of involvement and detachment: part of the incredible ritual, yet separate from it.

When the smith had dealt with all of my body parts like a smithy banging shapes out of metal, he laid the body next to the fibres and appeared to weld all the pieces together once more. Finally, gripping the network of fibres, he applied the hot poker from the furnace and seared a line right down the length of the spine. Working like a weaver, he plunged the fibres in and out of the body to form a web of light that penetrated through and beyond the boundaries of the skin. The entire procedure had been a terrible and a beautiful vision and though I felt no emotion, my thoughts seemed to soar with the enormity of it. I lost all sense of time. I did not know whether I had floated near the roof of that Underworld cave for seven heartbeats or seven moons.

Gradually I became aware of a sucking sensation and I fell backwards, plunging down as in a sudden awakening from a dream.

Then I slowed and came to rest gently. I felt a pounding in my chest and after a moment I realised that it was my heart beating. I was back in my body. Almost immediately I was swept from the rock and thrown across the cave; the bright orange light went out like an extinguished candle, I was crammed into the darkness of the tunnel and then I smelled the freshness of the night air. I opened my eyes but could see nothing; they were still adjusted to the orange light of the cave. But the fresh smell of grass filled my nostrils like a perfumed candle and I buried my face gratefully into the sopping night dew. After a short time I raised my head and looked around. I was lying on the grass, near the wildfires and Wulf was sitting in silence, watching me.

'Welcome back!' he chuckled.

I pushed myself up to a kneeling position. I felt better than I had for days; the light-headedness was gone completely.

'The dwarf has strengthened your body,' he said, sounding delighted. 'You are now ready to seek a guardian spirit.'

I looked down at my hands. In the firelight they looked unchanged and bore no sign of having been strengthened.

I did not know whether I had really encountered the dwarf, or whether it had been a dream. I had come to accept that spirit forces were entering my life, but the Underworld experience had been so unbelievably fantastic that I had to doubt it.

'Wulf, did I meet the dwarf in a dream?'

As soon as I asked the question, I knew the answer I wanted to hear. But Wulf took a long time to answer.

'If you can dream, then you can see the spirits,' he said eventually. 'Waking life wallows in the indulgences of the word-hoard. Words spin webs of deception and delusion. They shape and falsify our experience of wyrd to serve the human masters of fear and vanity. In dreams, however, words serve the true images of wyrd. In dreams the things we meet, even our enemies, tell us the truth, for in dreams we meet souls freed from the fears and foibles of Middle-Earth. Dreams offer a fragmentary glimpse of the spirit-world. To enter the sorcery of wyrd one needs only to dream.'

I felt a sudden, devastating disappointment. I wanted fervently to believe that the dwarf had been something more than merely a figment of my night-time imaginings.

'Can I never do more than glimpse the world of wyrd in dreams?' I said sadly. 'Is that all there is?'

I saw Wulf smile.

'Brand, do not doubt that you journeyed to the Underworld, and the welders of wildfire have given you great powers. Do not doubt that and you will be able to use those powers.'

My heart quickened. 'Now?'

He nodded.

'Will you show me?'

Wulf pulled me to my feet and I stood for a few moments, trying to regain my sense of balance. My body felt very strong but strange, as if my centre of balance were lower, and yet I felt taller. I lifted up my tunic and explored my body with my hands; it did not feel any different and was still covered by the dried layer of paste Wulf had applied after the encounter with the Wyrd Sisters.

'Is the green substance still affecting me?' I asked, remembering the strange sensations that had followed Wulf's treatment.

Wulf shook his head emphatically. 'You have slept for a night, a day and into another night. The protective salve no longer has potency.'

He was crouching near one of the fires, scrutinising me with half-closed eyes and smiling.

'Brand, you are producing a vast quantity of life-force and your body can now contain it without bursting into flames. Your shadow-soul is projecting a spirit-skin of vibrant colour and potency and may be able to journey to the spirit-world to recover your soul. But first you need the assistance of a guardian spirit to accompany you, and before that you must learn how to use your fibres.'

Wulf stood and walked over to me. 'Take off your clothes,' he said.

I looked at him in surprise. 'All of them?'

He nodded and, eager to begin, I stripped off my clothes and heaped them in a pile on the grass.

'Shoes, too,' he instructed.

I unstrapped my shoes and added them to the heap.

'Close your eyes,' Wulf said softly.

I stood on the grass between the shelter and the river, in the space lit by the two wildfires, and closed my eyes.

'You are at the centre of a web of power which extends to all worlds.' Wulf's voice came from behind me now. 'The dwarf has granted you the power to travel along those fibres to the far reaches of the web: the world of the spirits. Your fibres are passing right through your body, strong as welded spears. Stand quite still and you will feel them vibrating, pulling and pushing your body.'

I stood absolutely motionless, but I could feel nothing unusual. Occasionally Wulf adjusted my stance, lifting an arm further from my body, slightly changing the crook of my elbow, pulling my shoulders lower.'

'Soon you will be able to feel the fibres trembling,' he whispered.

My skin tingled slightly, but I felt nothing that might be trembling fibres.

'Wulf, I cannot feel a thing,' I confessed at last.

'Keep still. Keep your body aware,' he replied softly. 'It will happen.'

I could hear the cackle and spit of the fires and a distant owl hooting somewhere in the forest. The night air was warm and a sudden light breeze stroked my bare skin. Suddenly, to my surprise, I heard Wulf chuckling.

'The breeze you feel is the trembling of your fibres,' he said quietly.

I was awe-struck. The breeze took on a totally new significance and almost immediately I realised that it was coming not from one direction, but was swirling around all sides of my body at once.

'Do not be fooled by the gentleness of the fibres,' Wulf

murmured. 'Every day we adapt and adjust to the caresses without being aware of it. We listen to them, feel them, have our thoughts and moods changed by them. And although the fibres usually speak in a whisper, never forget that they can rage and, in a twinkling, can tear you apart.'

I was fascinated by the lilting quality of Wulf's voice; it seemed to fade in and out, along with the gentle gusts of breeze.

'Now wait for a stronger pull,' Wulf said. 'Keep your eyes closed and wait for a pull along a fibre. When you feel it, follow it.'

The breeze ruffled my hair and the sensation was exquisite, as if each hair was moving separately. Suddenly a very different sensation replaced it; I felt firm pressure in the small of my back, and for a moment I thought Wulf had pushed me. But then I heard his distant voice.

'Keep your eyes closed. Follow the pull of the fibres.'

I stood still for a moment, confused that I had felt a push whereas Wulf repeatedly referred to my being pulled along a fibre. I did not know whether the push was the kind of signal I was expected to feel. Then a sharp tug pulled me from the waist and I started walking across the grass. My eyes were tightly shut, but I could tell by the brightness on my eyelids that I had walked between the two wildfires, in a diagonal direction up the slope. Although I could not see where I was going, I walked quite rapidly with an uncanny sense of confidence, exactly as if Wulf were guiding me by pulling on my belt from the front. I slowed momentarily, wondering whether to look.

'Keep walking,' Wulf hissed, and I was startled to hear that he sounded to be at least ten paces behind me.

I sailed over the bumpy grass, propelled by the breeze and pulled from the front, and then the direction changed; the breeze gusted strongly from my left side and I was pulled from the right. Excitedly, I began to sidestep to the right.

'Keep the strength of the fibres in the middle of your back,' Wulf said, from somewhere in front of me.

I walked in rapid bursts of small steps and found that by making fine adjustments to my posture and direction, I could keep the strength of the fibres at my back. It was exhilarating. I felt that I had given up control over my movement and that the fibres were guiding me, taking care of me.

Abruptly the breeze died down and whispered contentedly in the grass. The pulling sensation disappeared. I stood motionless, eyes still closed and heard Wulf trotting to my side.

'Open your eyes,' he instructed.

I looked directly in front of me and saw that I was standing on the very edge of the river. The fibres had stopped just before I stepped off the bank into the water.

Wulf directed me back towards the fires. 'Now that you are able to heed the trembling of your fibres, the next step is to learn to leap along your fibres. Once you can do that, you will be able to leap into the sky, and journey with your guardian to the spirit-world.'

Wulf moved our clothes to the back of the clearing, then scooped up a large pile of dark green leaves and dropped them on to the flames. The two wildfires hissed and glowered and great clouds of green and orange smoke poured through the vegetation and billowed across the clearing. The area was plunged into darkness as the flames struggled beneath the leaves and the pouring columns of smoke reminded me of the steaming cauldrons I had seen in the Underworld.

'Follow me,' Wulf ordered, backing away from the fires. At the edge of the clearing he hesitated for a moment, then launched himself towards the flames, sprinting at least twenty paces and then leaping at such a height over the fires that he completely disappeared into the clouds of smoke. He seemed to have cleared both wildfires with his jump, but I could no longer see or hear him from where I stood. I even thought that he might have landed in the trees beyond the fires, though that hardly seemed credible.

Then I heard Wulf calling to me to jump.

I backed away from the fires towards the spot from which he had begun his run. Some of the leaves on the wildfire nearest to me sagged into the flames and dense smoke crackled and swirled into the night air. I ran towards the fire as fast as I could, slammed my left foot hard on the ground and leapt into the smoke with my eyes tightly shut. For a brief instant I sailed through the air, then opened my eyes the moment my leading foot hit the ground. My bare feet skidded across the grass and I slammed on to my back perilously close to the river.

Wulf helped me to my feet and wordlessly led me back towards the fires.

'Jump along your fibres,' he admonished, lining me up about thirty paces from the nearest fire. 'Wait until you see a fibre shimmering above the fire, then project your body along it.'

I closed my eyes and waited, but nothing appeared. I could feel the breeze on my bare skin, but no pulling sensation from the stomach. After a time I admitted to Wulf that I could not see anything that looked like a fibre. Perhaps the fall had upset me. I felt that it was useless to continue, for we would be waiting in vain for the rest of the night.

'Try again,' he insisted. 'Close your eyes and look for the fibres in the blackness.'

Sighing in resignation, I shut my eyes tightly. Almost immediately I glimpsed a shining line of light shooting away from me over the fire like a silver rainbow. I felt sure that I would lose the image if I opened my eyes, so I stood absolutely still and watched the fibre in the darkness of my eyelids. It pulsed like a beating heart and I thought I could feel it tugging me near my navel. Suddenly a breath of wind whipped across my chest and something pulled me forward on to my toes. I opened my eyes and the fibre glowed red, clearly visible, arcing high through the clouds of smoke. Without hesitation I sprinted hard towards the flames, bounded upwards on the fibre and shot over the wildfires as if carried by a storm-wind high above the smoke-belching leaves. Then I dropped like a stone and landed in a crumpled heap. I rolled on to my back just in time to see Wulf sailing over me and disappearing into the shrubbery beyond the edge of the clearing.

I was getting shakily to my feet when Wulf bounded to my side. He put an arm around my waist and led me slowly back into the clearing.

'You are doing well, Brand,' he said excitedly. 'But you lost concentration. You must keep your whole being focused on the fibres — keep them in your vision all the time. This is no task for a mind that flickers like a candle.'

Wulf drew me to the back of the clearing, pointed towards the fire and then ruffled my hair playfully.

'Right over the fires into the trees!' he chuckled.

I closed my eyes.

This time I had waited only a short time when I suddenly staggered forward, sucked by a swirling wind that cut cold across my stomach; then I ran towards the nearest fire with long, bouncing steps. Just before I reached the fire a fibre appeared before me like an incandescent rope reaching from my body into the sky, and I rose effortlessly from the ground. As I plunged through the smoke I thought I glimpsed at eye level the high branches of surrounding trees, then I hit the ground at tremendous speed. This time I absorbed the shock by bending my legs on impact. When I looked around in the darkness, I realised that I was sitting in a small patch of fern, by the edge of the clearing and at least ten paces from the second fire.

Wulf ran up and pulled me to my feet. His expression was all the encouragement I needed: I knew that I was now jumping with my fibres.

* * *

I leaped repeatedly through the wildfire smoke, higher each time until, as dawn streaked the sky, Wulf called a halt and I sank to the ground on the river bank. My eyes streamed with tears from the acrid smoke and I was soaked with sweat from the heat of the fires and the exertion. Yet I could have got up and jumped all day if necessary. I had never before experienced such a sense of physical power and balance and I was totally elated.

I bent over the river bank and ducked my head in the water, then drank noisily from cupped hands. When I turned back towards the shelter, Wulf was stripping the leafy twigs from several long hazel boughs and then sharpening the end of each bough to a point. He embedded the sharpened end of nine boughs into the turf around one of the wildfires, forming a circle, then bent them over so that the tops met above the fire to form a conical shape. Lashing the ends together with rope, he worked with great rapidity and in short bursts of activity between repeated retreats from the heat and smoke of the fire.

When Wulf had finished, he collected my clothes and draped them over the conical frame. I walked up the slope to join him. He looked at me and winked broadly.

'It was a good night's work, Brand. You can now project your body along your fibres and the smoke has purified you. Once your clothes have been purified too, we shall go in search of your guardian spirit. If we are successful in that quest, you will be able to project your shadow-soul along your fibres, and journey to the spirit-world.'

I turned and looked across the river at the dawn sky; there were further impossible tasks to perform, but for now I gave thanks for the rising sun beaming golden arrows of light into the retreating darkness. Two nights had passed and I was still alive.

13

IN SEARCH OF GUARDIANS

AT DAYBREAK we left the camp and started walking towards the hills. I felt strong and the miles passed quickly beneath my feet, though my stomach fluttered with fear. I was no longer afraid of encountering the spirits, for that would be necessary if I was to live, but I was terrified of making a terrible error that would destroy all my chances of survival. Wulf had warned me that if I did not heed the messages of the spirits I would never retrieve my soul, and that despite the help from the Underworld smith of sorcery I could not exist for long with merely a shadow-soul. As I walked, I continually dwelled upon the possibility that I would fail to recognise my guardian spirit, or even that I would journey to the spirit-world and somehow still fail to recapture my soul.

I gazed up into the passing trees, trying to rid my mind of anxieties. They did not leave me, but gradually I became aware that it was an entirely different concern that kept my mind spinning: the growing intensity of my desire to encounter my guardian spirit and to succeed in my attempt to journey to the spirit-world. As soon as I realised the power of this desire, I knew it to be the true reason for my apprehension. Living under the threat of death had in some way diminished the importance of merely preserving my life at all costs. I needed my guardian spirit to take me to the spirit-world and I needed to journey to the spirit-world to retrieve my soul. But it was the wonderful nature of that adventure that consumed me, not the necessity for survival. I was being offered the opportunity to experience the secrets of Middle-Earth sorcery, and I was anxious to seize this chance to the very best of my ability.

Wulf always insisted that we walk in silence, but when we stopped at noon to rest I asked the question that had ridden in my mind since we left the camp.

'Wulf, how will I know when my guardian spirit has arrived? What will it look like?'

He stretched out on the grass, lying flat on his back. 'When the guardian spirits manifest themselves to you they could appear in any one of a hundred guises. It could be a worm or a bear, insect or wolf, a mighty oak, even a pebble. And although there will be one guardian spirit for you, it may not necessarily appear alone. You will have to be open to every conceivable possibility.'

My heart sank. Wulf had confirmed my worst fears and I was sure that I would commit a major error and seal my own fate.

After a short silence Wulf's warm, infectious chuckle broke into my thoughts and he reached over to clap me playfully on the shoulder.

'You will recognise your guardian spirit, have no doubt,' he said cheerfully. 'The guardians are like shadows: visible outside your body, but forming an inexorable link with you. The essence of your guardian spirit already resides with you; that is why you will instantly recognise it when it appears.'

'The guardian spirit is inside me?' I was surprised.

'Everyone has the essence of their guardian spirits within them, but very few people know how to manifest their guardians and how to use them. The secret of the guardian spirits lies in the ability to extend the self beyond the boundaries of the physical body and to shoot along the lines of power into other worlds. The same ability applies to the guardians: if they can be projected into the world outside the body, they make available untold powers, they advise and protect you, they are with you whenever you need them.'

Wulf rolled on to his side, facing me, propped up on one elbow.

'Your guardian spirit will guide you to the spirit-world and leave you in the correct place, a place where you may begin to seek your soul. But you will journey to the spirit-world using your own power. There will be no protective salves, spearwort drinks or wildfires, and no Wulf to watch over you, for I shall leave you alone on the hills to summon your guardian spirit. You must journey along your fibres of power, projecting your shadow-soul along them just as you jumped along the fibres over the wildfires. But if your guardian spirit arrives, it will help you by journeying with you, perhaps even lending you its physical form. Your guardian spirit is for you alone and it will be with you all of your life. In fact, if you should ever see your guardian spirit leaving you, then you will know that death is imminent.'

I had been hanging on Wulf's every word, striving to ensure that I missed nothing that might help me succeed in this task; now I tried to question him further, but he placed a forefinger to his lips, then stood and stretched.

'The time for talking has ended,' he said, smiling. 'All your questions will be answered when you reach the spirit-world.'

* * *

It was late in the afternoon before Wulf led the way on to a narrow ridge which climbed out of the woods into the bracken-covered hills. Shadows raced up the hillside after us and the sinking sun warmed my back. We stopped at the top of a small rise and Wulf pointed towards the crest of the hill, far above us.

'There, Brand, at the burial mound of the giants, we will seek your guardian spirit. It is a place of immense power. From within that burial mound, the Wyrd Sisters weave the webs of wyrd.'

I followed his pointing finger and saw for the first time the tip of an enormous burial mound squatting on top of the hill—its grass-covered bulk, high as a barn, dominating the skyline. Until now the mound had been invisible, hidden by the brow of the hill. I shivered involuntarily.

'We are heading for that promontory,' he added, moving his finger to indicate a flat ridge directly beneath the mouth of the mound.

To reach the ridge we had to climb hard, grabbing for foot- and hand-holds and scrambling up escarpments of crumbling chalk rock. When we finally reached the ridge, I crawled away from the edge and lay down to get my breath. Above and behind us loomed the mouth of the burial mound, facing into the valley. All around the small plateau, stiff, stubby fingers of rock-plants rustled in the breeze.

Wulf was crouching at the edge of the ridge, on a rocky spur projecting out from the hillside. He turned and silently gestured for me to join him. I moved cautiously towards him, sat several feet from the edge and inched my way forward onto the rock, settling into a slight depression in the ground which gave me some small sense of security.

The view was breathtaking. The distant hilltops shone with the soft glow of the setting sun and cast deep shadows over the forest stretching out below us. The sun hovered just above the lip of the world and as I looked towards it, the entire landscape shattered into shimmering streaks of light. The effect was exhilarating.

'Brand, when your guardian has arrived, this is the point at which you will leave for your journey to the spirit-world. With your guardian, you must jump off this precipice on a fibre and your shadow-soul will fly.'

Very slowly, I leaned forward and peered over the edge. Below, water seemed to gush from some hidden spring out of the hillside and tumbled, spun and cascaded down the almost sheer cliff to disappear into the gathering shadows of the river valley.

Suddenly I felt dizzy. In panic I gripped the rock with both hands and leaned back, away from the edge. Then I felt Wulf right behind me, holding my shoulders firmly.

'Stay where you are,' he whispered urgently. 'This is a place of power. Feel the power with your body. Grip the rocks with your fibres.'

Wulf continued to hold me while I sat on the edge of the precipice. Gradually I became aware of a strange feeling. The crashing sound of the water became transformed into a bodily sensation, as if it were coming up through the hillside and setting up a vibration deep inside me.

The sun set very slowly, finally dipping below the distant stubble of tree-tops in a blaze of orange. The light faded and the moon appeared above us like a silver ghost. Wulf began to talk, softly.

'When I leave you, Brand, you must sing for your guardian spirit. You must draw your spirit to you along your fibres by singing your own song. That way the guardian spirit will find you.'

I looked at him, startled. I desperately wanted to do as he said, but I did not know how. I had no idea what to sing. I started to protest, but Wulf interrupted.

'Sing your own song, Brand. Do not worry about the words, just make the sounds that come to you. The spirits will understand.' He gripped my arm. 'You must do it, Brand. You must! If you do not sing, you will see only visions of death. You must sing to replace this bleak prospect with the ecstasy of the spirits. I cannot tell you what to sing, or how to sing. It is *your* guardian spirit we are seeking. It must be *your* song.'

I felt cheated. Wulf had not even hinted that I might have to sing and because I did not have appropriate words or sounds already learned, I was thrown into confusion.

'The songs you need are within you,' Wulf insisted, in a mixture of exhortation and encouragement. 'You will know the words when the time comes, for the essence of your guardian spirit is already within you. Float your word-hoard on the waves of wyrd; the power to release your guardian spirit lies within you alone.'

Suddenly Wulf laughed unexpectedly and the sound startled me.

'Relax,' he said. 'You are tying yourself in knots with tension. Relax and your guardian spirit will cut through the fog of your life like a sunbeam.'

I looked at Wulf and tried to smile, but I was so nervous I could not control my face. I felt my cheeks quivering and trembling.

Wulf chuckled merrily. 'You look like an owl trying to devour its prey,' he said. 'I believe the owl spirit must have chosen you.'

I laughed nervously. It felt wonderful to laugh and tension drained from me. I began to think that perhaps I could do it. Perhaps the words would come to me when I needed them.

Suddenly Wulf fell flat on his back and uttered a strange, long scream, 'Haaayeeee . . .' from deep within his throat. I stared at him through the soft dusk haze, paralysed by fear. I could not move.

Wulf had adopted a rigid posture on the ground, his feet

tucked back far under his body, a gurgling sound coming from his throat. Then his whole body trembled, he seemed to force himself slowly into an upright sitting position, spat hard onto the ground and swung his face towards me. His eyes looked large and wild, watching me almost with bewilderment like a scared animal.

'Your spirits will soon be here,' he rasped, his jaws opening and shutting with a strange, snapping motion. 'The spirits will soon be here, and I must leave you. Sing, Brand. Sing!'

He reached out and squeezed my arm, once, hard. Then he was gone. He disappeared so abruptly that I did not see him leave. I peered towards the shrubbery at the edge of the ridge, but the moon slipped behind clouds and I was looking at shifting shadows. I sat alone in the gathering darkness.

For a time I sat motionless. The hilltop was silent. I could hear not a sound, save for the gentle murmur of the breeze. Then, quite abruptly, the sky was lit again by pale moonglow and at that instant I shivered violently as if I had suddenly grown cold. The air around me was mild, but my body was strangely chilled. I stood and began clapping my arms around me to beat some warmth into my body, then I began running in small circles and gradually I felt better. The movement felt very good, but whenever I stopped I became extremely agitated and my body itched and twitched uncontrollably. I jumped about in the moonlight for a long time, until the sweat dripped from my face and I could hear my breath coming in hoarse, rasping gasps. I became fascinated by the rhythmic sound of my breathing and then I began to grunt with each breath. The sound was comforting. Each time I breathed out, I added louder voice to the gasp and after a while the grunting sounds came very freely, like the monotonous barking of a dog. Spellbound by the sounds, I began to vary the sound —breathing out with a groan, a gasp, a shriek. The sounds seemed to take over from me, varying themselves, rising and falling in pitch, now louder, now quieter, echoing around the ridge as the night closed in.

Suddenly I stopped. I could hear a voice singing and turned around to look for Wulf, but the ridge was deserted. Alarmed, I dropped to a crouch and stared wildly into the darkness, the

singing louder and closer now. With a sense of shock, I realised
that my lips were moving. It was my voice I could hear – I was
singing my song.

At first I did not know what I was singing. The words forced
my mouth and lips into a rhythm, my tongue into a shape. The
words sang through me. Sometimes the sounds I made frightened
me and I would grip the ground with my fingers and wait for
them to pass. Other times, the sounds were soft, sylph-like and
melodic. Then after a time I heard words I understood, though
their meaning was still a mystery.

> *Earth-cooler is the power*
> *who covers the sun like a shield,*
> *And allows the spirits protection*
> *to travel here on the wind.*
> *All-wise maiden who sits at Earth's rim,*
> *Knower of secrets, guardian of runes,*
> *From you flows swift the shuttle.*
> *In your hands the reel is turned*
> *And the copper shafts clatter,*
> *The silver comb resounds,*
> *and the fibres of wyrd are woven.*
> *Wind-weaver at Earth's rim,*
> *send the power of guardian spirits,*
> *send the sleep-bringer and dream-spinner,*
> *to guide me to the land of spirits,*
> *and show me the wonder of wyrd.*

I sang softly for a long time, well into the night. I had stopped
singing long before I realised it and just sat in stunned silence.
The singing had had a devastating effect on me, as if I had
opened myself to the entire world and no longer had any secrets,
any memories of which others knew nothing, even any identity
as a person. It seemed as if I had told everything in my
interminable song and there was nothing else of importance left
in my life. I felt utterly exhausted. Then something much worse
happened. Slowly, with the stealth of an assassin, the realisation
crept upon me that I had failed. I had sung my song and my
guardian spirit had not come to me. The full realisation hit me
like a dagger in the heart and I crumpled to the ground in a heap.

Far into the night, alone on the ridge, I wept bitterly and prepared to die.

Eventually I stopped and rolled over on my back, all energies completely and utterly spent. My stomach ached and I rubbed it gently with my right palm. A warm, good feeling crept over me, or rather it emanated from my stomach and coursed through my body and along my limbs, making my fingers and toes tingle. I could hear my breathing, slow and steady now, as if I were sleeping. But I knew that I was not sleeping, for my mind was sharp and alert.

Suddenly the sky was split in two by a flash of lightning and the land rumbled with answering thunder. Rain began to drizzle, then sleeted down, the wind blowing it directly into my face. Lightning flashed again across the sky and thunder growled menacingly. But this time it did not stop: the thunder kept rumbling, rolling and groaning. The very air around me seemed to take on the scent of danger and I began to feel very afraid. Water poured down my face and ran in a thin stream off the end of my nose; I wiped my face with my wet sleeve and peered around the ridge for shelter but I could see nothing: I was looking into a cloak of water. Then the long, continuous painful rumble of thunder seemed to roll up the hill and I could feel the ground trembling beneath my feet. Absurdly I braced myself against the rocks, trying to stabilise the ground, breathing in panic-stricken gasps. Desperate for shelter, I remembered the burial mound above the ridge and squinted up at the rocky entrance squatting on top of the hill: it glared silently into space, hoarder of souls from ages past and now, according to Wulf, witness to the weaving of the Wyrd Sisters. I took a few steps towards the rear of the small plateau, beneath the mound, and it disappeared behind the brow of the hill. The thunder boomed again and without hesitation I began to climb the rocks towards the entrance to the burial mound. I was doomed already and had nothing to lose. I feared nothing. In the moonlight, footholds materialised and disappeared just as quickly; twice I almost fell and my fingers ran wet with blood from gripping sharp edges. I struggled on to the top of the hill and crept closer to the mound until I could make out the entrance. Moonlight glinted off a pile of flint rocks, their bases buried by grass, moss and ferns. I crawled in amongst the boulders which formed the entrance and crouched down for shelter. The wind moaned through the gaps between the rocks and I flattened myself back against them and waited for the storm to die down.

The night sky was blanketed by fast-moving, swirling grey cloud which blotted out the moon. As I watched the clouds forming, I realised with an eerie sense of dread that the shine on the rocks was not moonlight but soft light chinking between the rocks, apparently coming from inside the mound. And what I had taken for the sound of wind through the rocks became voices, muffled and wailing. Mesmerised by the slits of light, I stood upright and crawled over rubble deeper into the rocky entrance. The light and noises stopped suddenly, though the wind howled around me and ghost-like storm clouds blanketed the moon completely. I peered through the cracks in the rock, but could now see nothing. I pressed my ear against the entrance, but no sounds rose above the wind. Then the wind seemed to change direction and suddenly I heard all the noises of a weaving room; clanking, thumping and bumping, whirring and clacking. I stooped, and peered through a crack between the rocks blocking the opening. Then I saw a most astonishing sight; I was staring into a high-vaulted chamber, well-lit and stacked with flax-lines, spindles, reels, yarn-winders, stoddle, beams, press, comb, weft, wool-comb, roller, cranks, shuttles, seam-pegs, shears, needles, beaters – in fact, everything that could be associated with looms and weaving. I struggled to get a clearer view, and then I saw them.

Three women were sitting at a large loom, busily weaving. All three had their backs to me, but I could see that they had long hair hanging loosely and were wearing white tunics or robes. I knew they were the Wyrd Sisters. They were weaving on upright looms, with clay loom-weights tightening warp threads and a weighted iron weaving sword for beating up the surface of woven material. But as I stared through the gap at the looms, things began to change. The strands of the loom glistened in the soft light and with a wave of revulsion I realised that they were human entrails. The clay loom-weights turned into men's heads and the shuttle was a blood-stained arrow.

Suddenly, the sounds stopped. I looked at the women and my heart stopped too. All three were staring directly towards me.

With a shriek I scrambled away over the rocks and tried to climb quickly down the precipice, kicking wildly for footholds, gasping and rasping for breath. Half-way down, I fell. The drop seemed to last an age and then I crashed into shrubbery where I lay very still for a moment, hardly daring to move. The only sensation I had was as if someone was pulling on my stomach very hard. I eased myself up and slowly crawled out of the shrub. I closed my eyes and shook my head to clear it, and it was then that I realised why my stomach felt strange: with a thrill of understanding, I realised that I had fallen along a fibre, and that was what had saved me.

The rain had almost ceased and lay in the air like a heavy mist. The sky began to clear. The moon eased into view and poured wet, twinkling light down through the mist. I looked into the shrubbery from which I had just crawled. The moonlight illuminated the leaves, glistening wetly and, as I watched, I suddenly realised that one of the shiny leaves had become detached and seemed to be shining directly at me. I stared at it in fascination. The bright spot began to grow in size and intensity and I had to squint to keep it from blinding me. Suddenly it disappeared and another equally bright spot replaced it, just a few inches to the right. Then, in an instant, I realised that I was looking at a hawk, a beautiful, powerful bird. It was perched on a branch, perhaps four feet from the ground, its eyes glittering as it turned its head to look at me. As I watched it, I began to tremble with excitement, until my body fluttered like a leaf in the wind.

The hawk glided silently from the branches and perched on the edge of the precipice. Slowly, I walked towards it, my heart hammering in my chest. Above the river, huge clouds rolled through the grey sky, twisting and turning, watching my every movement. Then they eased away again from the moon and the river shimmered far below like a bejewelled belt of silver lying across the forest.

I stepped on to the rocky spur and stood next to the hawk which stood motionless, waiting for me. My guardian had arrived and I knew what I must do. I took ten steps backwards, shut my eyes tightly and looked into the darkness. Almost immediately I saw a fibre, arcing skywards high over the valley towards the horizon. I took a deep breath, opened my eyes, launched myself towards the precipice and jumped.

14

A SORCERER'S SOUL

I SOARED over the edge of the precipice, felt the ground drop away beneath me and then began to plummet out of the sky towards the river far below. Tumbling and spinning, clutching at the air, glimpsing the river rushing up to meet me, I knew I would surely die. Suddenly my arms trembled violently and I stopped spinning. My arms trembled again and I soared through the air, the wind whistling and whining around me and I realised I was climbing into the sky. My body felt as light as a feather, and every time I trembled my arms, the river valley dropped further into the distance. I had an exhilarating, intoxicating sensation of speed and I pushed my head further forward to cut into the wind.

The moon seemed bright as the noon sun and far below in the river valley I could see movement everywhere, as sharply and clearly as if it were taking place on the back of my hand. Trees jerked around in the night wind, the river surged and poured down the valley like a living, breathing creature and everywhere in the clear spaces in the forest small nocturnal creatures scurried about in the moonlight.

I stretched my arms and immediately soared higher on the wind, flying north towards Earth's Rim like an arrow shooting through the sky with no earthly impediments to surmount. I followed the twisting line of the river, far below, until it broke up into tributaries and poured into the sea. I headed out over sea lying black and deep far below, white foam-flecked waves sparkling in the moonlight. But as I sped through the sky the sea took on a deep green hue and I could see fish swimming below the surface, each shining brightly like a jewel.

Then my body shuddered and for an instant I seemed to meet some distant part of myself—a falling, spinning, Middle-Earth-bound aspect of me. It felt like a pinprick of pain and immediately I lost height; then the wind caught my wings, I soared upward and the contact was gone.

Eventually I reached land again, a familiar landscape although I could not remember having been there before. Each landmark pulled at a chord of recognition as I swept over Grassy Inlet, climbed above Boundary Ridge, across Monster's Pit, through the Ivy Grove, then flying high to clear Eagle Ridge, plummeting and skimming over the ford in the Wooded Hollow and the Lily Brook, soared again to clear Middle Ridge and dropped once more to pass above the Giant Crab Apple Tree. Every feature of the landscape seemed to connect with some deep, forgotten memory which did not quite return but signalled in my mind that it was there.

Then I sped towards some hills and each time I topped one hill, a taller one rose in the darkness and I had to beat my wings powerfully in order to climb higher and higher. Finally, looming ahead above the creeping mists of dawn was a mighty mountain, the top lost in clouds, its sides coated with heavy forest. When I reached the lower slopes I glided down to land lightly in the branches of an ancient oak. I knew that I had journeyed into the spirit-world.

Looking up, I could see higher peaks covered with snow. In the other direction, down the mountainside, the distant forest lay blue in the light of early dawn. Directly below the oak tree, a narrow path led through the trees and up towards the top of a small rise. I decided to follow the path and trembled my wings, but nothing happened. Puzzled, I trembled them again, harder, but lost my balance, tumbled from the branches and landed sprawling in the grass, realising without surprise or concern that I was back in my usual body. I crawled to my feet unhurt and began walking up the path. The trees looked silvery as they caught the first glimmers of dawn sun, and the path was slippery with dew.

Soon I crested the small hill. The track sloped down towards a valley, cutting through the trees straight as a furrow from a giant's plough. I stopped and gazed down the path. A short bow-shot distance down the path a small cottage or hut nestled half-hidden in the trees, roof-thatch dipping low to the ground, smoke rising from the smoke-hole and curling away in the early morning breeze. The cottage fitted so perfectly with the surroundings that it slipped into invisibility, then back into sight with the tricks of the dawn light.

I strolled slowly down the hill towards the tiny building. I did not feel afraid, but my heart raced with excitement. Ducking under a low porch, I knocked on a heavy oak-plank door. There was no reply and no sound of movement from within, so I cautiously lifted the latch and pushed open the door. Inside the light was soft, the smell of wood and straw inviting as I stepped onto the threshold. The walls were hung with domestic utensils: cauldron, kettle and ladle sat near the burning fire and in one corner a wooden, iron-ringed tub, a cheese vat and a small pile of punnets. At the back of the room, raised from the earth floor by a low shelf, were stacked bags, sieves, a flour basket, honey-bin and yeast boxes. Down a side wall ran a raised platform with a mattress. The room was generously scattered with benches and stools and two fine, high-backed chairs were tucked neatly under a low table. Above the table a lantern hung from the central beam. It was all simple, basic and beautiful. I walked to the table and sat down in one of the chairs to wait.

Soon I heard footsteps. I sat very still and then in the open doorway a woman appeared, carrying a pail of water. She was the most enchanting woman I had ever seen; hair golden as harvest, part-braided but wind-blown under a leather headband, hazel eyes bright and sparkling; as soon as she saw me she smiled broadly, her teeth white and prominent.

'Hello, Brand.'

I was astonished to hear her speak my name and to hear her treat my presence as normal, expected, welcome. I knew now that I had seen her somewhere before, long ago, though I could not think where.

The woman swept into the room, took off a light, butter-coloured cloak and hung it on a wooden peg behind the door. Then she sat on the chair opposite me and arranged her long tunic over her knees. Her eyes were devastating and I could not take my gaze from her.

She smiled again, a little shyly and I realised that I was staring; I looked away quickly, blushing with embarrassment.

'How did you come to know my name?' I blustered clumsily.

'Woden pointed you out to me on your first night in the forest,' she replied pleasantly, her voice warm and slightly husky, her gaze direct. 'Since then I have watched you. Habrok the Hawk, your guardian spirit, surveyed your progress each dawn and reported to me. The moon watched over you by night and the sun tracked you by day. At dusk and dawn I listened to your activities from the rivers and streams. I have been here far longer than you realise, Brand. Ever since Woden marked you out on your first night in the forest.'

I believed her. I knew that she spoke the truth.

'Who are you?' I asked, staring at her again.

'Are you hungry?' she said, raising her eyebrows.

I nodded eagerly. I was not at all hungry, but I was willing to do whatever was necessary to prolong my time with her. The woman rose from the table and spooned some hot oatmeal from a pan over the fire. I noticed that she wore fine shoes of kid buckled with silver, though her tunic was simple. She lifted a stone at the back of the room and from a space dug in the floor she brought out a pitcher. Placing the bowl of oatmeal on the table, she poured creamy goats' milk from the pitcher.

I began to spoon the oatmeal slowly, making a special effort to eat neatly.

The woman sat down again. 'Brand, we must determine what it is you wish to know,' she said gently, holding me with her eyes again.

I did not know what to answer. I did not know who she was or what she could tell me. Suddenly it struck me that she might be a spirit or even a goddess and I knew immediately what she meant.

'I am here to learn about the ways of wyrd,' I said, after carefully swallowing my mouthful.

She giggled suddenly, surprisingly. In contrast with her honey-voice, her laugh was light and child-like and I loved the sound of it.

'Wulf said it all started with the giants,' I said awkwardly, desperate to establish the fact that I was not completely ignorant.

The woman laughed again, lightly, her teeth shining. She unhooked a rabbit-skin bag from her belt and placed it on the table, then got up from her chair and went to an oak chest, opened the lid and took out a white linen cloth. I pushed my bowl to one side and watched her closely.

She opened the cloth and spread it over the table. I noticed that she wore rings on all the fingers of her left hand; plain gold bands, several on each finger. Her hands were exquisite.

The woman sat in her chair and produced from the rabbit-skin a collection of small wooden sticks. She laid them on the white cloth and I gasped when I saw them. They looked just like the rune-sticks I had cut myself, which Wulf had broken and buried in the ground days ago. I could see the crudely cut marks; they were definitely my sticks, though they all looked as if they had never been broken.

I looked back into the woman's eyes.

'Are you going to foretell my future?' I asked eagerly.

She shook her head. 'I know the fates of all men and women, for I can read their threads of wyrd,' she said. 'But I do not prophesy. Your future is for you to live, not for me to tell.'

She picked up the pile of rune-sticks and tossed them in the air. When they fluttered and bounced back on to the white cloth, nine of them landed face upwards; seven were face down. The woman began to pick up the rune-sticks that faced upwards, beginning with those in the middle of the cloth and working out towards the edge. Reaching again into her rabbit-skin, she placed an empty rune-stave on the table, then slipped from a sheath at her belt a small, highly decorated knife with a thin, sharply pointed blade. With the knife she carved into the blank stave all the runes that had landed face upwards and as she carved, she spoke.

'I have learned all there is to know about the runes. I know how to cut them, how to read them, how to stain them and how to prove them. I know also how to evoke them, how to scare them and how to send them.' She glanced up at me, her eyes clear and compelling. 'Especially how to send them,' she repeated.

She pointed to the first rune she had carved: 'You must learn to become invisible and to melt into the air like morning mist. I shall teach you.'

She pointed to the second. 'But you must first know about the Beginning. You must know that in ancient days there existed nothing, neither sand nor sea, earth nor sky. There was only a mighty void with two contrasting regions, flame and frost; and these two together create the worlds. You must know the secrets of the mighty void.'

Her tongue slipped between her teeth as she looked closely at the next rune.

'The One who ruled from the Beginning had twelve names: first Allfather, second Lord of Hosts, third Lord of the Spear, fourth Smiter, then All-Knowing, Fulfiller of Wishes, Farspoken, Shaker, Burner, Destroyer, Protector and Gelding. I know the significance of each of those names and each one takes a lifetime to tell. You shall learn them all.'

She placed her finger on the fourth rune she had carved and I watched her face in wonder. She was utterly compelling and I soaked up every word she uttered.

'The next rune tells that it is Frostyfax who each morning sprinkles Middle-Earth with dew from his bit; he is Night's horse. Day's horse is Shinyfax, who illumines all the earth and sky with the light from his golden coat. You shall learn how to ride these two mighty steeds through the Underworld, Middle-Earth and into the Spirit-World.

'These other runes will grant many powers; of healing and recovering the souls of the sick; of blunting the edges of enemy swords, be they metal or sharp tongues.'

She finished carving the sixth rune and moved to the seventh:

'This seventh rune will empower you to free yourself from the bonds of evil sorcerers by smashing open the fetters of spells or catching a flying arrow aimed at your heart, be it feather-flighted or evil-minded action. An eighth rune teaches you to work with wildfire – to make it, to use it, to know it. And a ninth, to turn the hate of a person to love. These are powers, granted to you by the runes, that I can teach you if you wish to stay.'

I swallowed hard. I knew that I should be seeking my soul to save me from certain death, but I knew also that I wanted more than anything to learn the secrets of which she spoke. If I did not search for my soul, I did not know whether I would survive long enough in this world of spirits to learn all of the powers granted by the runes, but I could make a beginning. I had come this far, endured this much and I wanted to know the ways of wyrd.

'I am here to recover my soul, which was captured by the spirits,' I said, my voice shaking. 'Without my soul I will die, for my body cannot survive long with only a shadow-soul. But I may never find my soul, whereas I *have* found you. I will stay. I wish to learn.'

She watched me closely, her eyes seeing all.

'You would follow these teachings sooner than recover your soul? You would choose wisdom and death over assured life?'

I swallowed hard again and nodded. I had experienced wonderful things with Wulf and the prospect of learning more meant more to me than years of ignorant life.

She smiled radiantly and looked at me with moist eyes.

'You need do no more,' she said. 'I know these secrets; I have been taught by the spirits. And you shall know them too, for they are already yours. I am your soul.'

I was stunned. I gazed at her in utter amazement.

'When you return with me to Middle-Earth, I shall be within you. The secrets will be yours.'

'How can I do that?'

She laughed suddenly, her mirth bubbling like a spring. She was a most powerful woman: a strange and alluring combination of child, lover and mother. She reached out, took my hand and led me from the cottage into the trees at the back of the house, where a broad stream whirled rapidly down the hillside. A large, fallen oak stretched from the bank into the middle of the wide stream, like an unfinished bridge. The woman pointed to the branches of the tree, hanging over the water like giant fingers.

'Move to the end of the trunk,' she murmured.

I climbed on to the horizontal tree. The base of the trunk was covered with stream-bank vegetation, but as I crawled along it the rough bark was dry and warm. I crept along the trunk until I was sitting in the branches, the stream gurgling beneath me. The woman followed nimbly and sat next to me. Slowly she drew her knife from the sheath.

'Bend over the water as far as you can reach,' she said, whispering hoarsely above the sound of the water.

I looked at her in confusion, and she indicated the downstream side of the tree.

'Bend your head over the water,' she instructed. 'You must leave a small sacrifice to the Spirit-World for the return of your soul.'

Her voice echoed in my ears, although she was still whispering. I held on to a branch and leaned my head out over the water. She grasped my hair and pushed my head further, and I clung desperately to the branches in order to avoid being pitched into the stream. Then I felt something cold and hard on my neck and I closed my eyes. A stinging stab of pain shot through my neck. I jerked involuntarily and felt something warm trickling wetly down. When I opened my eyes, I saw blood dripping from my neck into the water. The woman leaned right over me, watching the blood disappear into the stream. I heard her counting and when she reached nine, she spoke loudly:

'Water Spirit, take this sacrifice and depart with it. Let Brand and his Soul be reunited in return.'

Suddenly and silently she was in the water. I knelt in the branches of the fallen oak and watched her wade towards the middle of the broad stream. The water surged to her waist, but no higher. She turned to face upstream towards the mountain, raised her hands above her head and began to sink slowly, the water swirling and snatching at her long hair. Her head dipped under, followed by her hands.

I waited for her to re-emerge. An age went by and still she did not reappear. In sudden panic I stripped off my shoes and tunic, jumped into the water and started to wade towards the middle. Suddenly she rose from the water naked, her skin smooth and glistening. She seemed iridescent and it almost hurt my eyes to look at her. We embraced.

The ripple of water sent a thrill through me and the stream swept us off our feet and carried us along with the current. I rolled and glimpsed the side of the mountain towering above. The sight took my breath away; far above me on the mountainside loomed a gigantic face, the lustrous eyes fringed by a leather crown. It was the woman, in my arms and on the mountainside.

Her mouth pouted and a shower of brilliant stars poured into the stream like a waterfall and covered me like drops of spray which blinded me with their crystal radiance. The hissing sparkles filled my ears with an ecstatic sound like rushing wind and I thought to myself, 'This, too, is God's world: I have seen it for the first time.'

Then I felt an enormous impact, my knees and body buckled and I sank to the bottom of the water.

EPILOGUE

I FELT myself being dragged up through the water like a fish on a line and I exploded into the air with a mighty gasp. Someone hauled me out of the stream and I could hear my body slapping onto rocks, gagging, coughing and wheezing until I could breathe. I looked around for the woman but she was not there. Then I heard a movement behind me; with a shout I turned to greet her, but squatting behind me was the familiar figure of Wulf.

'Where is she?' I gasped.

Wulf smiled enigmatically.

'You have journeyed into the spirit-world and retrieved your soul, Brand.'

Then I remembered. Slowly I sank on to my back and wrapped my arms around my stomach. My soul was inside me and it felt wonderful. I lay there for a long time, coughing sporadically but feeling ecstatically happy. I could not talk and even if I had been able, I would not have known what to say, for no words could describe my experience. But I knew that I did not have to talk; Wulf knew where I had been.

The rosy-hued light told me that it was early morning and I knew it would be a warm day. Then I realised that I was naked. I looked at the river behind Wulf and suddenly I knew where I was. Stretching far above us was an almost sheer chalk cliff and a cascade of water showered down the side into the deep stream at the bottom. Near the top of the cliff I could see the lip of the ridge from which I had jumped with my guardian. My mind went back to the night of singing and all the anguish I had endured. I smiled happily to myself. I had succeeded in journeying to the spirit-world, I had recovered my soul and, most important of all, I had glimpsed wonders that I knew were the province of God Himself.

Wulf walked up to me and placed my shoes and tunic by my side. I smiled my thanks and dressed; he pulled me to my feet and we walked back through the sun-dappled forest towards the camp. At first I felt shaky and unsteady, but as the day wore on I began to feel supremely strong. By mid-afternoon we had arrived back at the shelter, and I felt tremendously better. I strolled down to the river to catch fish for supper while Wulf laid a fresh fire. Squatting on the familiar rock, I threw bait into the water. Slowly, carefully, lovingly, I reviewed in my mind the events leading to my journey to the Earth's Rim and the woman who had turned out to be my soul. And I knew that I had experienced the world of our Lord as never before; my love for Him filled my heart. But Eappa had been right; my personal mission in the forest of the pagans had brought me closer to the Almighty, though Eappa could never have guessed the nature of that experience.

At the end of the summer, I would have to return to the Mission and tell Eappa all I knew, though there was precious little of it which I could convey in words. But I could tell him that when the Word of Almighty God was spread in this forest it would fall on fertile ground, for the kingdom of the pagans truly contained spiritual secrets that were as much a part of God's world as the land from which we came.

When I had caught a fish, I cleaned and gutted it, then carried it up the slope to the fire-pit. Wulf wrapped it in leaves and pushed it into the glowing embers to bake.

Suddenly I noticed a neatly packed bundle near the entrance to the shelter and realised it contained my belongings. I turned to Wulf in surprise.

'I have finished my task,' he said quietly, looking at me with clear, kind eyes. 'I have served as your guide into our ways of wyrd and helped you to journey into the spirit-world. It is time for you to return to your masters.'

I was shocked. 'But Wulf, there are weeks yet before ships

anchor to avoid the cold clamp of winter. I do not need to travel
before the summer is spent.'

He smiled warmly.

'Brand, there is nothing more I can teach you. All the knowledge you seek is now within you. It will take you a lifetime to
learn the secrets in your soul, but you cannot learn them from
me.'

He leaned forward and rolled the cooking fish over with a
stick.

'I will guide you to a ship,' he said quietly. 'It will take only
two days and you can obtain passage back to your Mission.'

I looked down the slope towards the river. The warm day was
sinking into a soft dusk, gentle and subtle. I felt overwhelming
sadness. I did not want to leave.

Suddenly Wulf stood and disappeared into the shelter. When
he re-emerged he was carrying something wrapped in a piece of
linen.

'You may travel with me this summer if you wish,' he said. 'If
you do, I will not be your guide, for only you can find the knowledge within you. Or I can take you to the coast to find a boat. I
shall need your decision by dawn. In the meantime, here are
some things to help you in your decision.'

He laid the linen parcel on the grass in front of me and I saw
that there were two folded sides, each concealing an object. Wulf
flipped back both sides of the cloth simultaneously and I gasped
in amazement; lying on one side of the cloth was my bronze
crucifix, clean and shining and on the other, astonishingly, the
long knife forged by the dwarf of the Underworld with which he
had cut me to pieces. I would have recognised that knife
anywhere.

But I knew what I wanted to do; I did not need to ponder a
decision overnight. I reached out and picked up the crucifix,
kissed it and fastened it around my neck. Wulf looked down
quickly and started to wrap up the knife, but I put out a hand to
stop him. Then I picked up the knife and slipped it into my
sheath at my belt.

'I will stay,' I said happily. 'I am a servant of Almighty God,
but it is in the world of wyrd that I experienced His wonder.
There is time enough to return to the Mission. I wish to stay

here and get to know the secrets within me.'

Slowly, very slowly, a grin spread across Wulf's face. He started to chuckle, his infectious laughter bubbling out like water from a spring. I began to chuckle too, feeling a bond of brotherhood with Wulf – a bond that could never be broken. Our laughter splashed around the clearing and sent the crows wheeling out of the trees to speed away down river in a tumbling, twisting, zigzag flight. I watched the pattern of their flight and I understood.

BIBLIOGRAPHY

THE FOLLOWING list of references is intended to serve both as a bibliography of the main sources on which the research for this book was based, and as a guide to the literature for readers who may wish to pursue their own lines of enquiry into Anglo-Saxon and other traditions of sorcery. To keep the bibliography to manageable proportions I have listed only those Anglo-Saxon references which contributed directly in some way to the writing of this book, omitting the many more general works which provided invaluable background and perspective. Some of the references in this section include extensive bibliographies which will serve as guides to further reading.

The bibliography of comparative sorcery has had to be even more selective, for recent research specifically on shamanism and sorcery alone extends to several hundred articles. I have therefore listed only books which were of direct relevance to the preparation of *The Way of Wyrd*, and which together represent something of the wide range of subjects and disciplines which bear upon the investigation of sorcery. Again, many of these books have full bibliographies of recent journal literature.

ANGLO-SAXON SORCERY

Alcock, L. *Arthur's Britain*. Harmondsworth: Penguin 1971.

Alexander, M. *The Earliest English Poems*. Harmondsworth: Penguin 1966.

Anderson, G. K. *The Literature of the Anglo-Saxons*. New York: Russell and Russell 1962.

Bannard, H. E. 'Some English sites of ancient heathen worship', *Hibbert Journal*. 1945, XLIV, 76–79.

Barley, N. F. 'Anglo-Saxon Magico-Medicine', *Journal of the Anthropological Society of Oxford, 3*. 1972, 67–77.

Blair, P. H. *An Introduction to Anglo-Saxon England* (Second Edition). London: Cambridge University Press 1977.

Blair, P. H. *The World of Bede*. London: Secker 1970.

Bonser, W. 'The significance of colour in ancient and medieval magic, with some modern comparisons', *Man XXV*. 1925, 194–8.

Bonser, W. 'Magical practices against elves', *Folk-lore XXXVII*, 1926, 356–363.

Bonser, W. 'The dissimilarity of ancient Irish magic from that of the Anglo-Saxons', *Folk-lore XXXVII*, 1926, 271–88.

Bonser, W. 'Survivals of paganism in Anglo-Saxon England', *Transactions of the Birmingham Archaeological Society*. 1932, *LVI*, 37–70.

Bonser, W. 'Animal skins in magic and medicine', *Folk-lore LXXIII*, 1962, 128–29.

Bonser, W. *The Medical Background of Anglo-Saxon England*. London: Wellcome Historical Medical Library 1963.

Brandon, P. (ed.) *The South Saxons*. London: Phillimore 1978.

Branston, B. *The Lost Gods of England*. London: Thames and Hudson 1957 (reprinted 1974).

Brown, A. and Foote, P. (eds.) *Early English and Norse Studies*. London: Methuen 1963.

Bruce-Mitford, R. *The Sutton Hoo Ship-Burial*. London: British Museum 1972.

Buchholz, P. 'Perspectives for historical research in Germanic religion', *History of Religions*, 1968, *8* (2), 111–138.

Cameron, K. *English Place-Names*. London: B. T. Batsford 1961.

Chadwick, H. M. *The Cult of Othin*. London: Cambridge University Press 1899.

Chadwick, H. M. *The Origin of the English Nation*. London: Cambridge University Press 1907 (reprinted 1924).

Chadwick, H. M. *The Heroic Age*. London: Cambridge University Press 1912.

Chadwick, N. K. 'The monsters and Beowulf' in P. Clemoes (ed.), *The Anglo-Saxons*. London 1959.

Chaney, W. 'Paganism to Christianity in Anglo-Saxon England', *Harvard Theological Review LIII*, 1960.

Chaney, W. A. 'Aethelberht's code and the King's number', *American Journal of Legal History VI* 1962, 151–177.

Chaney, W. A. *The Cult of Kingship in Anglo-Saxon England*. Manchester: Manchester University Press 1970.

Clemoes, P. (ed.) *Anglo-Saxon England 3*. London: Cambridge University Press 1974.

Cockayne, T. O. *Leechdoms, Wortcunning and Starcraft of Early England* (three volumes). Rolls series 1864–6. Reissue London: Holland Press 1961.

Cohen, S. L. 'The Sutton Hoo Whetstone', *Speculum* 1966 *XLI* 466–470.

Colgrave, B. *The Venerable Bede and His Times*. Newcastle-upon-Tyne 1958.

Crossley-Holland, K. *The Norse Myths*. London: Andre Deutsch 1980.

Daiches, D. *A Critical History of English Literature* (Volume 1). London: Secker and Warburg 1963.

Davidson, H. R. E. 'The hill of the dragon: Anglo-Saxon burial mounds in literature and archaeology', *Folk-lore LXI*. 1950, 169–184.

Davidson, H. R. E. 'Weland the Smith', *Folk-lore LXIX*. 1959, 145–159.

Davidson, H. R. E. *Gods and Myths of Northern Europe*. Harmondsworth: Penguin 1964.

Davidson, H. R. E. 'Scandinavian cosmology' in C. Blacker and M. Loewe (eds.), *Ancient Cosmologies*. London 1975.

Dickins, B. (ed.) *Runic and Heroic Poems of the Old Teutonic Peoples*. London: Cambridge University Press 1915.

Dickins, B. 'Yorkshire hobs', *Trans. Yorks. Dialect. Soc., XII*, 1942, 9–23.

Dickins, B. 'English names and Old English heathenism', *Essays and Studies* (of the English Association) *XIX*, 1934.

Dickins, B. 'Runic rings and Old English charms', *Archiv. Stud. neuron. Sprachen., 67.* 1935.

Dillon, M. and Chadwick, N. *The Celtic Realms*. London: Weidenfeld and Nicolson 1967.

Dobbie, E. van K. *Anglo-Saxon Minor Poems* in Krapp, G. P. and Dobbie, E. van K. (eds.) *Anglo-Saxon Poetic Records: 6*. New York: Columbia University Press 1942.

Dumezil, G. (edited and translated by E. Haugen). *Gods of the Ancient Northmen*. London: University of California Press 1973.

Eliade, M. *Occultism, Witchcraft and Cultural Fashions*. Chicago: University of Chicago Press 1976.

Elliott, R. W. V. *Runes: an Introduction*. Manchester: Manchester University Press 1959.

Gardner, J. *Grendel*. London: Andre Deutsch 1972.

Garmonsway, G. N. *Beowulf and its Analogues*. New York: E. P. Dutton & Co. 1969.

Garmonsway, G. N. (ed. and translator). *The Anglo-Saxon Chronicle*. London: J. M. Dent 1972 (first published Everyman 1953).

Gelling, M. 'Place-names and Anglo-Saxon paganism', *University of Birmingham Historical Journal, 8.* 1961–62. 7–24.

Gordon, R. K. *Anglo-Saxon Poetry*. London: J. M. Dent 1954 (reprinted 'Everyman' edition 1977).

Grattan, J. 'Three Anglo-Saxon charms from the Lacnunga' in *Modern Language Review XXII*, 1927, 1–6.

Grattan, J. H. G. and Singer, C. *Anglo-Saxon Magic and Medicine*. Wellcome Historical Medical Museum, Oxford University Press 1952.

Greenfield, S. B. *A Critical History of Old English Literature*. University of London Press 1966.

Grendon, F. 'The Anglo-Saxon charms', *Journ. Amer. Folk-Lore XXII*, 1909.

Grimm, J. L. (edited and translated by J. E. Stallybrass). *Teutonic Mythology* (four volumes). London: Bell 1880–8.

Hachmann, R. (translator J. Hogarth). *The Germanic Peoples*. London: Barrie and Jenkins 1971.

Harrison, R. 'The beginning of the year in England c. 500–900' in P. Clemoes (ed.), *Anglo-Saxon England 2*. London: Cambridge University Press 1973.

Harrison, M. *The Roots of Witchcraft*. London: Muller 1973.

Hill, T. D. 'The aecerbot charm and its Christian user' in P. Clemoes (ed.), *Anglo-Saxon England 6*. Cambridge: Cambridge University Press 1977.

Hodgkin, R. H. *A History of the Anglo-Saxons (third edition)*, (2 volumes). London: Oxford University Press 1952.

Howe, G. M. *Man, Environment and Disease in Britain*. Newton Abbot: David and Charles 1973.

Hunter, M. 'Germanic and Roman antiquity and the sense of the past in Anglo-Saxon England' in P. Clemoes (ed.), *Anglo-Saxon England 3*. London: Cambridge University Press 1974.

Kemble, J. M. *The Saxons in England* (volume 1). London: Longman, Brown, Green and Longmans 1849.

Kern, F. (translator S. B. Chrimes). *Kingship and Law in the Middle Ages*. Oxford: Blackwell 1939.

Kirby, D. P. *The Making of Early England*. London: B. T. Batsford 1967.

Kittredge, G. L. *Witchcraft in Old and New England*. Cambridge (Mass.) 1929.

Lester, G. A. *The Anglo-Saxons: How They Lived and Worked*. Newton Abbott: David and Charles 1976.

Magnusson, M. *Hammer of the North*. London: Orbis 1976.

Magnusson, M. and Palsson, H. *Njal's Saga*. London: Penguin 1960.

Magnusson, M. and Palsson, H. *King Harald's Saga*. London: Penguin 1966.

Magoun, F. P. 'Old English charm A.13', *Modern Language Notes 58*, 1943, 33–34.

Magoun, F. P. 'On some survivals of pagan belief in Anglo-Saxon England', *Harvard Theol. Review XI*, 1947, 85.

Maringer, J. 'Priests and priestesses in prehistoric Europe', *History of Religions, 17* (2), 1977, 101–120.

Matthews, C. M. *Place Names of the English-Speaking World*. London: Weidenfeld and Nicholson 1972.

Mayr-Harting, H. *The Coming of Christianity to Anglo-Saxon England*. London: B. T. Batsford 1972.

Meroney, H. 'Irish in the Old English charms', *Speculum, XX*, 172–182.

Morris, J. *The Age of Arthur: a History of the British Isles from 350 to 650*. London: Weidenfeld and Nicolson 1973.

Musset, L. (translator E. and C. James). *The Germanic Invasions. The Making of Europe A.D. 400–600*. London: Paul Elek 1975.

Myres, J. N. L. *Anglo-Saxon Pottery and the Settlement of England*. Oxford: Clarendon Press 1969.

Onians, R. B. *The Origins of European Thought*. London: Cambridge University Press 1954.

Page, R. I. 'Anglo-Saxon runes and magic', *Journal of Archaeological Association* (third series), XXVII, 1964.

Page, R. I. *Life in Anglo-Saxon England*. London 1970.

Page, R. I. *An Introduction to English Runes*. London: Methuen 1973.

Payne, J. F. *English Medicine in Anglo-Saxon Times*. Oxford 1904.

Quennell, C. H. B. and M. *Everyday Life in Roman and Anglo-Saxon Times*.

Reaney, P. H. *The Origin of English Place-Names*. London: Routledge and Kegan Paul 1960.

Renwick, W. and Orton, H. *The Beginnings of English Literature to Skelton*. Cresset Press 1952 (revised edition).

Robertson, D. 'Magical medicine in Viking Scandinavia', *Medical History, 20*, 1976, 317–22.

Runeberg, A. *Witches, Demons and Fertility Magic*. Helsingford 1947.

Ryan, J. S. 'Othin in England: evidence from the poetry for a cult of Woden in Anglo-Saxon England', *Folk-Lore*, 1963, 460–480.

Shook, L. K. 'Notes on the Old English charms', *Modern Language Notes, 55*, 1940, 139–40.

Singer, C. *From Magic to Science*. New York: Dover 1958 (originally published 1928).

Skemp, A. R. 'The Old English charms', *Modern Language Review, 6*, 1911, 289–301.

Smith, A. W. 'The luck in the head: a problem in English folklore', *Folklore, LXXIII*, 1962, 13–24.

Smith, A. W. 'The luck in the head: some further observations', *Folklore, LXXIX*, 1963, 396–398.

Stanley, E. G. *Continuations and Beginnings: Studies in Old English Literature*. London: Nelson 1966.

Stanley, E. G. *The Search for Anglo-Saxon Paganism*. Cambridge: D. S. Brewer, 1975.

Stenton, D. M. (ed.) *Preparatory to Anglo-Saxon England: the Collected Papers of Frank Merry Stenton*. Oxford: The Clarendon Press 1970.

Stenton, F. M. *Anglo-Saxon England* (second edition). Oxford: Clarendon Press 1947.

Storms, G. *Anglo-Saxon Magic*. The Hague: Martinus Nijhoff 1948.

Strutynski, U. 'Germanic divinities in weekday names', *Journal of Indo-European Studies, 3*, 1975, 363–84.

Stuart, H. 'The Anglo-Saxon Elf', *Studia Neophilogica*, *48*, 1976, 313–20.

Sturluson, S. (translator J. I. Young). *The Prose Edda*. Cambridge: Bowes and Bowes 1954.

Swanton M. (ed.) *Anglo-Saxon Prose*. London: Dent 1975.

Talbot, C. H. *Medicine in Medieval England*. London: Olbourne 1967.

Tatlock, J. S. P. 'The dragons of Wessex and Wales', *Speculum*, *VIII*. 1933, 223–235.

Taylor, P. B. and Auden, W. H. (translators). *The Elder Edda: A Selection*. London: Faber and Faber 1969.

Thun, N. 'The malignant elves', *Studia Neophilologica*, *41*, 1969, 378–396.

Todd, M. *The Northern Barbarians*, 100 B.A. – A.D. 300. London: Hutchinson 1975.

Tolkien, J. R. R. *Beowulf: the Monsters and the Critics*. London: Oxford University Press 1937.

Tolkien, J. R. R. Preface to *Beowulf and the Finnesburg Fragment*, J. R. C. Hall, revised by C. L. Wrenn. London: Allen and Unwin 1940.

Tolkien, J. R. R. *The Lord of the Rings*. London: Allen and Unwin 1968.

Turville-Petre, E. O. G. *Myth and Religion of the North*. London: Weidenfeld and Nicolson 1964.

Van Hamel, A. 'Odin hanging on the tree', *Acta Philologica Scandinavica*, 7, 1932, 260.

de Vries, J. 'Magic and religion', *History of Religions*. 1962, *1* (2), 214–221.

Wax, R. H. *Magic, Fate and History: the Changing Ethos of the Vikings*. Kansas: Colorado Press 1969.

Whitelock, D. *The Audience of Beowulf*. Oxford: Clarendon Press 1951.

Whitelock, D. *The Beginnings of English Society*. Harmondsworth: Penguin 1952.

Whitelock, D. *English Historical Documents*. London: Eyre 1955.

Williams, B. C. *Gnomic Poetry in Anglo-Saxon*. New York: Columbia University Press 1914.

Wilson, D. M. *The Anglo-Saxons* (second edition). Harmondsworth: Penguin 1971.

Wright, C. E. *The Cultivation of Saga in Anglo-Saxon England*. Edinburgh: Oliver 1939.

COMPARATIVE SORCERY AND RELATED READINGS

Blacker, C. *The Catalpa Bow: a study of shamanistic practices in Japan*. London: Allen and Unwin 1975.

Bleibtreu, J. *The Parable of the Beast*. London: Gollancz 1968.

Capra, C. *The Tao of Physics*. London: Wildwood House 1975.

Castaneda, C. *The Teachings of Don Juan*. New York: Ballantine Books 1968.

Castaneda, C. *A Separate Reality*. New York; Simon and Schuster 1971.

Castaneda, C. *Journey to Ixtlan*. New York: Simon and Schuster 19972.

Castaneda, C. *Tales of Power*. London: Hodder and Stoughton 1974.

Castaneda, C. *The Second Ring of Power*. New York: Simon and Schuster 1977.

Castaneda, C. *The Eagle's Gift*. London: Hodder and Stoughton 1981.

David-Neal, A. *Magic and Mystery in Tibet*. London: Abacus 1977.

De Mille, R. *Castaneda's Journey: The Power and the Allegory*. Santa Barbara, California: Capra Press.

Dobkin de Rios, M. *Visionary Vine*. San Francisco: Chandler 1972.

Edsman, C. M. (ed.) *Studies in Shamanism*. Stockholm: Almquist and Wiksell 1967.

Eliade, M. *Shamanism: Archaic techniques of ecstasy*. London: Routledge and Kegan Paul 1964.

Eliade, M. *The Forge and the Crucible*. New York: Harper and Row 1971.

Furst, P. (ed.) *Flesh of the Gods: the ritual use of hallucinogens*. New York: Praegar 1972.

Graves, R. *The White Goddess*. London: Faber and Faber 1952.

Grof, S. *Realms of the Human Unconscious*. New York: Viking 1975.

Halifax, J. *Shamanic Voices*. New York: Dutton 1978.

Halifax, J. *Shaman: the Wounded Healer*. London: Thames and Hudson 1982.

Hand, W. C. (ed.) *American Folk Medicine*. Berkeley: University of California Press 1976.

Hardy, A. *The Living Stream*. London: Collins 1965.

Hardy, A., Harvie, R. and Koestler, A. *The Challenge of Chance*. London: Hutchinson 1973.

Harner, M. J. (ed.) *Hallucinogens and Shamanism*. New York: Oxford University Press 1973.

Harner, M. *The Way of the Shaman*. New York: Bantam Books 1982.

Hesse, H. *Steppenwolf*. New York: Bantam 1969.

Hesse, H. *Demian*. London: Panther Books 1969.

Huxley, A. *Doors of Perception*. London: Chatto 1968.

Huxley, F. *The Invisibles*. London: Rupert Hart-Davis 1966.

Huxley, F. *The Way of the Sacred*. London: Aldus Books 1974.

Inglis, B. *Natural and Supernatural*. London: Hodder and Stoughton 1977.

Inglis, B. *Natural Medicine*. London: Collins 1979.

Jung, C. G. *Memories, Dreams, Reflections*. London: Routledge and Kegan Paul 1963.

Koestler, A. *The Roots of Coincidence*. London: Hutchinson 1972.

La Barre, W. *The Peyote Cult* (Revised Edition). New York: Schocken 1969.

La Barre, W. *The Ghost Dance: the origins of a religion*. New York: Dell Books 1972.

Laing, R. *The Politics of Experience*. New York: Pantheon 1967.

Laing, R. D. *The Voice of Experience*. London: Allen Lane 1982.

Larsen, S. *The Shaman's Doorway*. New York: Harper and Row 1976.

Lessing, D. *Briefing for a Descent into Hell*. London: Jonathan Cape 1971.

Lewis, I. M. *Ecstatic Religion*. Penguin 1971.

Lilly, J. C. *The Center of the Cyclone*. New York: Julian Press 1973.

Lommel, A. *Shamanism*. New York: McGraw-Hill 1967.

Masters, R. E. L. and Houston, J. *The Varieties of Psychedelic Experience*. New York: Dell 1966.

Masters, R. E. L. and Houston, J. *Mind Games*. New York: Viking 1972.

Myerhoff, B. *The Peyote Hunt: the Sacred Journey of the Huichol Indians*. Ithaca, N.Y.: Cornell University Press 1974.

Naranjo, C. *The One Quest*. New York: The Viking Press 1972.

Noel, D. *Seeing Castaneda*. New York: Putnam's Sons 1976.

Ornstein, R. *The Psychology of Consciousness*. New York: Viking 1972.

Park, W. Z. *Shamanism in Western North America*. New York: Cooper Square 1975.

Rothenberg, J. (ed.) *Technicians of the Sacred*. Garden City, N.Y.: Doubleday 1968.

Sargent, W. *The Mind Possessed*. London: Heinemann 1973.

Sharon, D. *Wizard of the Four Winds*. New York: The Free Press 1978.

Targ, R. and Puthoff, H. *Mind-Reach*. London: Jonathan Cape 1977.

Tart, C. T. (ed.) *Altered States of Consciousness*. London: Wiley 1969.

Tart, C. T. (ed.) *Transpersonal Psychologies*. London: Routledge and Kegan Paul 1975.

Ullman, M., Krippner, S. and Vaughan, A. *Dream Telepathy*. New York: MacMillan 1973.

Waley, A. *The Way and its Power*. London: Unwin Paperbacks 1977.

Wasson, R. G. *Soma: Divine mushroom of immortality*. New York: Harcourt, Brace, Jovanovich 1972.

Watson, L. *Supernature*. London: Hodder and Stoughton 1973.

Watts, A. W. Tao: *The Watercourse Way*. London: Jonathan Cape 1976.

Weil, A. *The Natural Mind*. London: Jonathan Cape 1973.

White, J. (ed.) *The Highest State of Consciousness*. New York: Doubleday 1972.